MARCO

CARIBBEAN

Approaching it on a cruise vessel is already something special, because seeing it from the sea gives you entirely new views of your destination.
The variety of places to visit, the arts and culture, the country and its people – on a cruise you experience all the manifold aspects of travelling. Moreover, modern liners also offer entertainment and relaxation on board.
Bon voyage and ahoy there on your route around the Caribbean!

SYMBOLS

INSIDER TIP   Insider Tip

★   Highlight

☆☆   Scenic View

🌍   Responsible travel: for ecological or fair trade aspects

PRICE CATEGORIES RESTAURANTS

Expensive   over £10/US$13

Moderate   £5–10/US$6–13

Budget   under £5/US$6

Prices for a main dish and one non-alcoholic drink

DID YOU KNOW?
Timeline → p. 8, Art Deco District → p. 16, Slow rivers run deep → p. 19, Hemingway → p. 20, On the menu and on the street → p. 27, Travel with kids → p. 28, Nicely calcified → p. 32, Travel with kids → p. 34, Caution – Bearers of secrets! → p. 39, Travel with kids → p. 40, Local Specialities → p. 42,

CONTENTS

Spoil yourself → p. 43, Travel with kids → p. 44, Jamaican Legend → p. 48, Travel with kids → p. 55, Atlantis stone → p. 56, Come shake a leg → p. 59, Gum Jurassic → p. 60, At the drop of the bat → p. 71, Do you speak English? → p. 74, High-grade waste → p. 89, A riot of colour → p. 92, White Gold → p. 98,

Specialities → p. 100, Wild Whirlies → p. 106, Love song, anyone? → p. 111, Playful Pre-Colombians → p. 113, Witnesses in the jungle → p. 118, Rhythmical symbiosis → p. 122, Through sickness to fame → p. 138, Tasty fast foods → p. 140

MAPS IN THE GUIDEBOOK
(𝄞 1/A3) refers to the pull-out maps

INSIDE FRONT COVER:
The best highlights

INSIDE BACK COVER:
General map

The best MARCO POLO Insider Tips

Our top 15 Insider Tips

INSIDER TIP Swimming like the stars
Palm-fringed water, ambience with a touch of Venice – perfect backdrop for a little you-time → p. 17

INSIDER TIP Trusty cartilaginous fish
This is an absolute must-see: schools of rays glide through the waters of Gibb's Cay when there are boats in the vicinity (see photo above →p. 34

INSIDER TIP Ivan Chef Justo
In the cosy little top room near the beach road Malecón in Havana the *Ivan Chefs Justo* treats its fans to the imaginative culinary delights of a top chef → p. 42

INSIDER TIP For gourmets
It won't do your waistline any good, but it's too good to pass up: the finest chocolates, made with indigenous cacao – and you can even watch how they are made → p. 43

INSIDER TIP Bare coins
They once rested in the treasure chests of sunken ships; now they are sought-after souvenirs: In Georgetown, on *Grand Cayman*, real "pirate coins" are sold → p. 46

INSIDER TIP Mansion with a view
On a tour through the *Greenwood Great House*, you can admire the original furnishings and enjoy the fantastic view from the veranda → p. 49

INSIDER TIP Art and artists
The *Galería Bolós* in *Santo Domingo* delights with its unusual instinct for quality and originality. Whether it's carnival masks, wood carvings, colourfully painted ceramics or paintings, nothing is mass produced → p. 56

INSIDER TIP How about a few dunes?
In the nature park *Las Dunas de las Calderas*, on the southern coast at Las Salinas, the dunes are higher and longer than the whole town

and form an impressive barrier to the Bahía de las Calderas → **p. 56**

→ **p. 56**

INSIDER TIP **Voodoo pictures and sculptures**
The *Haitian Caraibes Art Gallery* in the Dominican Las Terrenas has a fine selection of unusual craft objects – even its own house cigar brand → **p. 59**

INSIDER TIP **Begone, woe!**
A drink that does the trick: You should try at least one "painkiller" on Jost van Dyke, the north-western island neighbour of Tortola → **p. 70**

INSIDER TIP **Raise your glasses!**
In the *Musée du Rhum Saint-James* in Ste-Marie on Martinique you can also conclude your visit by sampling the high-octane export winner → **p. 80**

INSIDER TIP **Nature's medicine chest**
The healing powers of the Aloe vera are acknowledged in Europe as well. Here you can learn about the production of beneficial products (photo below) → **p. 96**

INSIDER TIP **Among ageing hippies and rockers**
Todo Santos is the fishing town loved by bohemians and individualists: here on the peninsula of Baja California, the dream of stress-free living has come true → **p. 113**

INSIDER TIP **Rapture of the deep**
Diving into the dark: Take the submersible into the nether regions that normally remain hidden from human eyes → **p. 124**

INSIDER TIP **Monkey and wild cat sanctuary**
In the *Centro de Rescate Jaguar*, on the Caribbean coast, injured, orphaned and confiscated wild animals are cared for → **p. 129**

CAST OFF

DISCOVER THE CARIBBEAN!

"Oh, island in the sun ..." Do you remember this line, which used to be sung by Harry Belafonte, the son of a Jamaican mother and a farther from Martinique? Do visions of an everlasting sun, shimmering blue and green waters, beaches of powdery white sand, hills planted with sugar cane and dense rainforests sometimes rise before your inner eye? Can you hardly wait for your ship to take you out to this fantastic world of large and little islands stretching south from Florida to the Central American coastline like a string of pearls, alive with a rich variety of plants and animals, that's just waiting for you?

The island Harry Belafonte was singing about may have been fictional, but he could have been thinking of any of the Caribbean islands you will visit on your cruise through this dream world. Perhaps you will even hum this tune when your ship takes to the sea from Florida, for example, towards the unique island world. And while you are in the area – not to worry, Captain Jack Sparrow will in all probability not be lying in wait for you – why not take along some

Photo: Blue sea, white beaches, palms: a Caribbean cruise promises you this and much more impressions of *Florida* itself? *Miami* is awaiting you not only with outstanding museums, but also with its unique Art Deco district and, in the vicinity, with the Everglades and the *Florida Keys* – this string of islands will prepare you for what is still in store.

On your voyage you could also stop over on the *Bahamas*, south of Florida, as well as on the *Turks and Caicos Islands* to the south-east. Another place worth your while is the coast of *Mexico*; here you will – for the first, but certainly not the last time on your trip – encounter the legendary Maya, whose traces remaining today testify to the highly developed culture of this people that inhabited Central America long before the American continent was discovered by Columbus.

Most certainly the *Greater Antilles* will be on your itinerary; culturally these can be split into several nations: *Cuba*, the *Dominican Republic* and *Puerto Rico* are as Spanish as they became after their discovery some 500 years ago, although since the end of the 19th century Puerto Rico belongs to the USA. *Jamaica* and the *Cayman Islands* belong to the English language area – just like the Bahamas, which are geographically not really part of the Caribbean – while French is spoken in Haiti. In Cuba, which is gradually opening up to the West, you travel into the past in American street cruisers, in Jamaica the typical reggae sounds are waiting for you, and the Cayman Islands are much more than just a tax haven. The inhabitants of all these islands are a diverse pot-pourri of peoples: There are the descendants of African slaves, of the emigrants from almost all countries in Europe, Chinese, Indian and Arabic businesspeople, of South and North Americans and the first Amerindian inhabitants of the islands. Religious, social, cultural or political barriers are rare, and you will very often encounter friendly people and a relaxed way of living. And this continues on the *Lesser Antilles*: while for example *Barbados* or, just off the coast of Venezuela, *Trinidad and Tobago* bear the stamp of the British, on *Martinique* or *Guadeloupe* there are also French enclaves that are actually overseas French territories. The Dutch also left their tracks in the Caribbean, for example on the *ABC islands* Aruba, Bonaire and Curaçao. Here you can sip the eponymous liquor, but the Carib-

> **Ancient Maya temples, laid-back reggae sounds and language diversity**

Since 1000 BC
Indians from the Orinoco area occupy the Caribbean from north to south

250–900 AD
Classical era of the Maya culture in southern Mexico; around 900 the Maya leave their city states

1492–94
In 1492 Columbus lands on Guanahani (probably San Salvador, Bahamas). He crosses the Caribbean four times and is followed by Spanish settlers

16th–18th century
Freebooters carry on their nefarious business between the islands of the Caribbean and are a major hazard to trading vessels

One of the many Caribbean paradise beaches: Bottom Bay on Barbados

bean is equally well known for its rum – this is its natural habitat, as the sugar (the indispensable ingredient) flourishes in the Caribbean climate. Perhaps you have the good fortune to interrupt your voyage on the coasts of *Colombia* in the north of South America and the Central American states of *Panama*, *Costa Rica*, *Nicaragua*, *El Salvador*, *Honduras* and *Guatemala* – countries that have not been focused on for nearly as long as the Caribbean islands, but nevertheless offer unique experiences of nature, from rainforests to volcanoes.

17th–18th century
French, English and Dutch settlers move into the Caribbean. Using African slaves, the islands experience an economic boom by producing sugar.

1814/15
Treaties of Paris: Cuba, Puerto Rico and the eastern part of Hispaniola remain Spanish, Jamaica and the Cayman Islands remain British.

1834–63
The British, French and Dutch abolish slavery

1953–59
Revolution on Cuba; Fidel Castro takes over power

AROUND THE CARIBBEAN

WET PARADISE

Heights of 40 m and more are nothing special among the thousands of species of trees in rainforests, which occur in the Caribbean as well as in Central America and Colombia. In fact, this forest type hosts half of all the world's animal and plant species. In the jungle, life unfolds in 'storeys' – dark, high and very moist at the bottom, while life in the forest canopy has remained largely unresearched. The world's most stable, but also most sensitive ecosystem, millions of years old, has survived climate variations since the ice ages but is now threatened by mankind and the environmental influences it has brought about. As recently as 50 years ago, Costa Rica's rainforest (in the tropical lowlands) and in the cloud forest (above 1000 m) covered more than 70% of the country.

WELL CLADDED

Some enjoy it as a snack or a soup, others as jewellery: Despite numerous protection agreements and legislation, the eggs, meat and shell of tortoises are still being exploited and exported. Some animal species that have been around for 100 million years are nearing extinction. In Costa Rica they are being taken care of; several research stations investigate, mark and protect as well as nurture them. In both seas of the country, turtles swim ashore in their thousands when the moon is out and the tide high, laboriously crawl

In the Caribbean, dense tropical rainforests and wide dream beaches meet numerous objects bearing witness to former colonial masters

up the beach and dig 50 cm deep holes for their eggs. Some of these animals weigh several hundred kilos, and the nocturnal procedure is commensurately slow, allowing tourists – given certain precautions, such as no light or noise – to look on. In six to eight weeks, the sun incubates the eggs – if nobody has dug them up before then – and up to 100 little turtles struggle up through the layer of sand and head straight for the briny water. Many don't make it and fall prey to people, birds and fish.

DANCING ISLANDS

Spreading from the Greater Antilles, many musical styles and dances have conquered the world: the salsa from Puerto Rico, the rumba, cha-cha-cha and the son from Cuba. Accompanied by congas and rattles, son (Spanish for 'sound') is played in authentic bars in Cuba. Ska, reggae, soca and what has become known as Calypso hail from Jamaica. If there is going to be a dance hall session in the evening, enormous sound systems are already erected in bars and on the streets in the afternoon. Then ragamuffin, reggaeton and dance hall discs are mixed live by DJs and produced with spontaneous word plays, breaks and rewinds as a real sound storm. And lastly, the meringue hails from the Dominican Republic. As different as these musical styles may be, they have some unmistakable characteristics in common: they always mix African rhythms with European traditions in ever novel ways, often with a strong shot of North American pop music thrown in.

OF HOVELS AND PALACES

Little pastel-coloured wooden houses, known as "gingerbread houses", can be found all over the Caribbean islands, whether English, French or Spanish-speaking. Besides these, there are the stately homes of the colonial bosses: urban palaces in the 16th and 17th century Spanish style, with elaborately decorated arcades, columns and enchanted courtyards, can be found especially in the old-town neighbourhoods of Havana, Santo Domingo and San Juan. The mansions of the sugar and coffee plantations are also worth visiting.

SWEET GOLD

Sugar ruled the political and social life on the Greater Antilles and in other parts of the Caribbean for a long time. The owners of the large plantations mostly lived in their home countries

Colorfully painted houses along the streets of San Juan on Puerto Rico

and left their properties in the hands of managers. The laws, however, came from Spain, England or France and often had little or nothing in common with the needs of the plantation labourers. Wealth and power were in the hands of a few families, but were created by African slaves, whose health (and, often enough, lives) were sacrificed to the luxury of their masters. Only the cultivation of sugar beet in Europe heralded the collapse of the Caribbean plantations, and thereby the end of slavery.

THE LAND OF CURLY LOCKS

You'll find them in European and US metropolises too: the Rastafarians with their long, matted dreadlocks. And reggae, their music, has spread all over the world, played by the greats of pop music such as Bob Marley, the Wailers or Peter Tosh. But the home of their religion is Jamaica; that's where reggae comes from and where the dreadlocks curled for the first time. For the Rastafarians, the concept "Babylon" comprises all that is wordly, corrupt and sinful, the state and the established church, in short everything and everybody that does not fit into the sole saving belief in Haile Selassie Ras Tafari, the "lion of Judah" and former emperor of Ethiopia.

PIRATES OF THE CARIBBEAN

In the 16th, 17th and 18th centuries the freebooters, pirates and buccaneers were the true masters of the Caribbean Sea. The Spanish galleons, well laden with gold and silver treasures from the New World, were a welcome and often also an easy prey. Henry Morgan, Blackbeard and all the other audacious rascals did not hesitate to attack and plunder even the well-fortified cities on the islands. Piracy only came to an end when the major European powers stopped using these undisciplined and unreliable bands as accessories in the proxy wars they fought against one another in the Caribbean.

WHIRLING WINDS

Not every hurricane season brings the Caribbean a dangerous tropical storm, and not every hurricane that makes landfall on one of the islands causes huge and dramatic damage. But the number and force of the storms has distinctly increased in recent years. It seems that the further to the north the islands lie, the higher the probability of hurricanes. The Windward Islands and Barbados, for example, are hit less often than the Leeward Islands and the Virgin Islands. Most of the traces of severe storms are cleared away within a few weeks.

WELL TRAVELLED

Christopher Columbus was the first European tourist in the Caribbean. Today every local patriot on the Antilles can tell you when and on which of his voyages Colón (that's the Spanish version of the name) sighted or "discovered" the islands. The alleged facts are not historically proven, as ships' logs, reports by eye witnesses and the maps of the age of discovery are not dependable sources. But maybe it is not really all that important... What is certain is that his name has become established even in South America: after all, Colombia bears his name, thereby honouring this Italian explorer who carried out his Castilian instructions.

FLORIDA/USA

The American Way of Life is a mythical mixture of freedom and leisure, sun and sand, optimism and openness, the quick buck and instant gratification.

Nowhere else in the USA do you experience this lifestyle as distinctly as in Florida, the Sunshine State. So when you stop over here on your cruise, immerse yourself in this very particular culture. On the same latitude as North Africa, a satisfied Florida happily basks under a mostly blue sky. However, Florida offers more than pure sun: world famous art museums and galleries, wonderful conservation areas, excellent cuisine and the best theme parks of all! We guarantee you won't be bored during your visit to Florida – that's a promise.

MIAMI

Beach in front, wilderness behind, sun above and a whirlpool of life in the middle – that's Miami, the pivot of an entire continent.

In this city the English-speaking USA meets Spanish-speaking Latin America. Miami is a phenomenon: the city is just about 100 years old. At breakneck speed, it has developed from a fishing hamlet into an international banking centre a tourism metropolis and lately also a trendsetter in the world of art. When the East Coast Railroad arrived in 1896, the rise into the stratosphere of wealth took off. The most exotic metropolis in the USA is a cultural patchwork. Together with Cubans, im-

More than just the proverbial sun: in Florida you also experience art and culture and an exciting nature

migrants from El Salvador, Nicaragua and Colombia make up more than 50 per cent of the population. This has turned Spanish into the second lingua franca and given the city, which for many years was mainly a wintering place for Americans from the north, a new look and feel. Miami's architecture, on the other hand, borrows more from a Mediterranean style, which has persisted in upper-class neighbourhoods such as Coral Gables and Coconut Grove.

SIGHTSEEING

BASS MUSEUM OF ART
The most striking feature of this exciting collection, which forms part of the *Miami Beach Cultural Park*, is the interesting changing exhibitions with unorthodox modern art and architecture. *Wed/Mon 10am–8pm | Admission $10 | 2100 Collins Av. | Miami Beach | thebass.org*

COCONUT GROVE
This suburb in the south of Miami cen-

ART DECO DISTRICT

Pastel shades in tropical colours. Streamlined facades and ornaments borrowed from the Aztec and Mayan style elements: with this combination, the architects of the Art Deco district created an American icon. It is due to the resistance of a single woman that the beautiful buildings have survived to this day: During the building boom of the 1970s, investors wanted to tear everything down. Thanks to Barbara Capitman, you can still wander through the hotel lobbies and admire the creativity of the designers of those days. Tours start at the *Art Deco District Welcome Center (Fri–Wed 10.30am, Thu 10.30 and 6.30pm | Price $25/£27.7)*. Here you can also get info about tours on your own *(Tue–Sat 10am–5pm, Sun until 7pm | 1001 Ocean Drive | Miami Beach | Tel. 1 305 6 72 20 14 | www.mdpl.org)*.

tres on the intersection of Grand Avenue and McFarlane Road, with its many bars and sidewalk restaurants. A two-minute walk away, hidden in a tropical thicket, Miami's oldest house (built in 1891) has survived floods and hurricanes. Protected as *Barnacle State Historic Site (Wed–Mon 9am–5pm | Admission $2/£2.6, guided tour $3/£2.4 | 3485 Main Highway)*, its spacious verandas recall a more leisurely era. Good place for a picnic! The shopping area Coco Walk *(3015 Grand Av./Virginia Street)*, especially the elegant mall streets of Mayfair *(Grand Av./MacFarlane Road)*, bustle with people of all cultures and colours.

CORAL GABLES (🛍 2/E1)
The formerly plushest part of Miami was built in the early 1920s. Magnificent boulevards, shady avenues with Mediterranean villas and perfectly manicured lawns: Miracle Mile, the elegant shopping street between Douglas Road and Le Jeune Road, is the showpiece of the suburb. Places of interest are the *Colonnade Building (180 Aragon Av.)* finished in cool marble inside; *Merrick House (Wed, Sun 1–4pm | admssion $5/£3.9 |*

907 Coral Way), the parental home of the builder of Coral Gables, George Merrick, as well as the ornate *Biltmore Hotel (1200 Anastasia Av./www.biltmorehotel.com)*, which opened in 1926 and offers its sometimes prominent guests tennis courts, a golf course as well as a polo field. On Sundays at 1pm you can take a INSIDER**TIP** free guided tour through the historic edifice.

FAIRCHILD TROPICAL GARDEN (🛍 2/E1)
Call it a feast for the eyes or sensory overstimulation: more than 5000 tropical plants in a single garden. *Daily 9.30am–4.30pm | Admission $25/£19.8 | 10901 Old Cutler Road | Coral Gables | www.fairchild garden.org*

HISTORYMIAMI (🛍 1/A3)
The history of the south-west of Florida, especially of Miami, the Keys and the Everglades, is displayed on two large storeys. Worthwhile and informative are the INSIDER**TIP** city tours offered by experts. *Tue–Sat 10am–5pm, Sun 12am–5pm | Admission $10/£7.9 | 101 W Flagler Street*

MUSEUM OF CONTEMPORARY ART (MOCA)

The renowned MOCA displays high-level modern as well as classical art. It owes its fame to the curator's feeling for new trends and talent. *Tue–Fri 11am–5pm, Sat 1pm–9pm, Sun noon–5pm| Admission $5/£3.9 | 770 NE 125th Street | North Miami | mocanomi.org*

PATRICIA AND PHILLIP FROST MUSEUM OF SCIENCE *(1/B–C2)*

The whole world of science presented interactively in a spectacular multi-storey building with open spaces. *Daily 9.30 am–5.30pm | Admission $29/£22.9 | 1101 Biscayne Blvd. | Coconut Grove | www.frostscience.org*

PÉREZ ART MUSEUM ★ *(1/C1)*

The grandiose Pérez Art Museum in the museum park has been the new cultural centre of downtown Miami since 2013. The spectacular building, designed by Herzog & de Meuron, accommodates especially international modern artists, including John Baldessari, Olafur Eliasson and Wifredo Lam. Every second Saturday and every first Thursday admission is free. *Fri–Tue 10am–6pm, Thu 10am–5pm, 1st Thu of the month 10am–9pm | Admission $6 | 1103 Biscayne Blvd.|Downtown|www.pamm.org*

INSIDER TIP RUBELL FAMILY CONNECTION

Often provoking, the Rubell family's collection of modern American art offers a unique cross-section of the country's contemporary art scene. Must see! *Wed–Sat 10am–5.30pm | Admission $10/£7.9 | 95 NW 29th Street | Miami Downtown/Wynwood Art District | rfc.museum*

INSIDER TIP VENETIAN POOL *(2/E1)*

In the 1920s a coral quarry supplied the material for this Venetian-inspired swimming pool, in which the Hollywood stars of the early days took their dips.

A riot of colour on Ocean Drive in the Art Deco district

MIANI

MIAMI

Feb.–April Tue–Sun 10am–4.30pm, otherwise Tue–Fri 11am–5.30pm, Sat–Sun 10am–4.30pm | Admission $15 | 2701 De Soto Blvd. | Coral Gables | www. coralgables.com

VIZCAYA MUSEUM AND GARDENS
Opulence from the times when the American anti-trust laws were still new and porous: The palatial villa, in the style of the Italian Renaissance, was the winter residence of the industrial magnate and art hobbyist James Deering, who made his fortune from agricultural machines. Its 34 rooms are furnished with antiquities from all over the world. Equally worth seeing are the expansive gardens of the 20,000 m² property. *Wed–Mon 9.30am–4.30pm | Admission $18/£14.3 | 3251 Miami Av. | Coconut Grove | www. vizcaya.org*

THE WOLFSONIAN-FIU
The private collection of Mitchell Wolfson jnr. is kept in a bunker-type edifice

Tasteful home for art:
the Vizcaya Museum

with Art Deco elements located in the heart of the Art Deco district. On display are design objects from the period between 1885 and 1945. The collections of the British Arts & Crafts movement and the Art Nouveau style in the Netherlands and Italy are of particular interest. *Mon, Wed, Thu, Sat 10am–6pm, Fri 10am–9pm, Sun noon–6pm | Admission $12/£9.15, Fri 6pm–9pm free| 1001 Washington Av. | South Beach | www. wolfsonian.org*

WYNWOOD
With street art *(www.thewynwoodwalls. com)*, street food *(www.thewynwoodyard. com)* and hip cafés, e.g. Dr. Smood *(2230 NW 2nd Av. | www.drsmood.com)*, Wynwood has become the hottest part of Miami in just a few years. Where until recently deserted warehouses were quietly decaying away, this area north of downtown now combines everything that is dear to today's trendies. It all started in 2002, when Art Basel set up a branch in Miami. Now some INSIDER TIP ▶ 25 galleries and about 20 restaurants, cafés and bars compete for the mainly young customers.

FOOD & DRINK

BARTON G.
That's entertainment: every meal is served in a highly unusual presentation. The accompanying cocktails have names such as 'Sin-Sation' or 'Buddhalicious', one dish is presented as 'Lured by Salmon'. The ambience is elegant. *1427 W | South Beach | www.bartong.com | Expensive*

THE WYNWOOD YARD
Top-notch street food: In a backyard in the hip Wynwood area, about a dozen chefs are showing off their idea of mod-

SLOW RIVERS RUN DEEP

That's the traditional view. But this does not always hold water - Florida's Everglades are not a marsh, but a river with an extremely low flow rate. And it is nothing less than 80 km/50 mi wide, but only 15 cm/6 in deep! Sedges and other water plants conceal not only the water, but also the extremely slow flow. As the elevation in the interior is only 3 m higher than that of the Gulf of Mexico, the water takes about a year to cover the distance (160 km/100 mi) to the sea. The bog and marsh landscape, interspersed with slightly higher forested islands and cut by natural water courses, Is considered a very sensitive ecosystem that is home to alligators, pelicans and rare fish species.

ern fast food. Try the Calypso spare ribs or Spanish-Asian rice bowls. This comes with live music and yoga in the open air. *56 NW 29th Street/The Lots | www.thewynwoodyard.com | Budget*

LIME FRESH MEXICAN GRILL
Lively restaurant of the chain represented by some Tex-Mex grills on the East Coast. Risk of burrito and fajita addiction! *3275 NE 1st Ave | Midtown | Tel. 1 305 7 89 02 52 | Budget/Moderate*

SHOPPING

AVENTURA MALL
For Americans, shopping is a substitute for culture. In this three-storey complex with 300 shops, shopaholics and bargain hunters can stock up on consumer goods – from surfer wear to designer skirts. *19501 Biscayne Blvd. | Aventura | aventuramall.com*

ESPAÑOLA WAY
Romantic shopping: where once there were brothels, you now find funky boutiques, beauty salons and shops for design accessories. Between Washington *Av. and Euclid Av. | South Beach*

LINCOLN ROAD MALL ★
A pedestrian zone seven city blocks long between Washington Av. and Alton Road in South Beach with more than 170 shops, 26 galleries and 48 restaurants and bars, some of which are outstanding. Street music, produce market *(Sun 9am–7pm)* and INSIDER TIP antiques market *(every 2nd Sun in winter)*. The aroma of café cubano reigns in the *Lincoln Road Café (no. 943)*, and gifted artists from all parts of the USA have studios in the *Art Center/ South Florida (800, 810 and 924)*. You can get the news *atlincolnroadmall.com* and a map at *www.lincolnroadmall.info.)*

WHERE TO GO

BISCAYNE NATIONAL PARK (*🕮 2/E1*)
95 per cent of the 9000 km² /347 mi² conservation area within sight of Miami lies under clear water. In a boat with a glass bottom, you can watch the fascinating underwater world with colourful fish and stately turtles without getting wet. *Biscayne Underwater Parks Tour Boat Office | Visitor Information | Daily 8am–5.30pm | Tel. 1 305 2 30 72 75 | www.nps.gov/bisc/index.htm*

FLORIDA KEYS

On the Florida Keys you enter a world with tropical flair and very laid-back residents. Here there is little that reminds you of the rest of the USA.

The islands form a 180 km/112 mi chain from the continent almost to Cuba, interconnected by the Overseas Highway, which has 42 bridges (including the 11 km Seven Mile Bridge) and allows vehicles to cross the open sea. A large number of the 1000 little limestone and mangrove islands are uninhabited. Where people live, they have made their mark on the islands by erecting wooden houses hidden in the shrubbery and pretty yacht moorings.

HEMINGWAY

Ernest Miller Hemingway (1899–1961) spent one of his most productive creative phases on Key West; during the 12 years he lived here, this is where he wrote, among others, "In a different country" and "A farewell to arms". In his novel "The old man and the sea" the author immortalised the Keys. Today his former living and working rooms are a museum. *Hemingway Home | Daily 9am–5pm | Admission $13/£10.3 | 907 Whitehead Street | www. hemingwayhome.com*

CONCH REPUBLIC

The Florida Keys islanders are one of a kind. In 1982 they even briefly seceded from the federation, because the federal police, in an attempt to catch smugglers, allowed them onto the continent only on presentation of their passports and was therefore treating them as foreigners. Washington eventually relented, but the distinct us-and-them feeling remained – as did the Secretary General of the Conch Republic, who likes to solemnly grant the citizenship of the Conch Republic. The Conch Republic *(www.conchrepublic.com)* still keeps a headquarters where interested people can apply for a passport at a fee of $100/£79.12.

COLOURFUL MIXTURE

The greatest diversity of characters is found at the extreme end, in Key West.

Chill and enjoy life – the Key spirit in the south of Florida is a totally unique sense of life under the tropical sun

This is where the so-called *conchs* (pronounced: Konks) live, oldtimers who call themselves after a type of shell, a large gay community, Cuban refugees, artists and students, all of whom are living the easy-going pace of the archipelago, the legendary *Key spirit*. But life never was hectic here, not even when Key West was a stop-over of the line ships under way to the Gulf of Mexico and the Caribbean and when fishermen, sponge divers and a pineapple factory boosted the island economy in the 19th century. There are still many houses from the early years, which give Key West its romantic character.

TRUSTY CARTILAGINOUS FISH

At first glance, Robbie's Marina in Islamorada is an angling operator like any other. However, the excited crowd at the jetty suggests that there's more

to it. It all started with Scarface, an injured tarpon (a species of cartilaginous fish), which Robbie nursed back to health and then released. But the released Scarface returned, with other tarpons in tow. Every day the visitors turn up at the end of the jetty with buckets of sardines to feed Scarface's heirs. Occasionally, the ever-hungry fish, up to two metres/six feet long, rocket out of the water, making the water boil.

SUBMARINE CONSERVATION

The best part of the 461 km²/180 mi² ★ John Pennekamp State Park, established in 1963, lies under water: a truly impressive panorama of nature with attractions such as the two and a half metres tall underwater statue Christ of the Abyss. The park has several beaches, mangrove forests and a coral reef aquarium.

TRAVEL TIPS

BERTHS

The Port of Miami has several modern cruise ship terminals. Taxis and car hire firms are available to incoming passengers in all terminals. There is a Metrorail station about 2.5 km/2 mi from the port. The Orange Line takes you to the city centre. The Coral Way Route of the Miami trolley line stops at the port about every 15 to 20 minutes.

CUSTOMS

The following may be taken into the US duty free: 1 l spirits, 200 cigarettes or 50 cigars. Many foodstuffs, especially fresh, may not be imported. The following may be imported into the EU duty free: 1 l spirits, 200 cigarettes or 100 cigarillos or 50 cigars or 250 g tobacco, 50 g perfume or 250 g eau de toilette and other goods (except for gold) to a total value of 430 euros or less than 300 francs in the case of Switzerland. Importing coral and alligator skin (belts, bags) into Europe is prohibited. For reasons of species protection, importing shellfish jewellery is not allowed either. Only three natural shells are allowed per person.

EMERGENCY SERVICES

Toll-free number for police and medical emergencies: tel. 911

HEALTH

The emergency rooms (ERs) of hospitals are obliged to treat all patients. Foreigners are asked for a credit card. Be sure to take out international medical insurance cover before embarking on your trip!

IMMIGRATION

The red, machine-readable passport is required. For newly issued passports, biometric data are also prescribed, otherwise a visa is required as for a stay of more than three months. Passports issued after October 2006 must, as so-called e-passports, also contain biometric data on a chip. Children must have their own passports. In addition, the electronic travel authorisation procedure ESTA is compulsory, which must be applied for online at least 72 hours before the journey starts (esta.cbp.dhs.gov/esta/). A fee is charged for the ESTA application since 2010.

MONEY, BANKS & CREDIT CARDS

Banks (usually Mon–Thu 10am–3pm, Fr 10am–5pm) do not exchange currencies, but they do cash traveller's cheques and pay cash on credit cards. Credit cards are the most popular means of payment. European cards may cause problems when for security reasons a postal code is requested. With the EC card you can also draw money at ATMs that accept Maestro.

TELEPHONE, MOBILE PHONE & WIFI

In the USA smartphones are used almost exclusively. All new-generation equipment bought in Europe also

Florida/USA

**Your holiday from start to finish:
the main information for your trip**

works on the US networks. The respective terms and conditions of the relevant rate will be sent to you by sms when you emigrate. Anyone who wants to can also buy data packages for internet use from their service provider. Like telephone calls, these are quite expensive, but incredibly practical.

In most spaces there is free WiFi; in some cases, you have to ask for a password *(WiFi code)*. The US country code is 001, followed by a three-digit area code. Calls within the USA, whether local or long-distance, start with the 1 followed by the area code and seven-digit number. The code numbers 800 and 888 are free. Calls to the UK: direct line 01144, then the area code without the 0 and the subscriber's number. Collect calls and calls with a phone card (obtainable free of charge from Telekom) at tel. 0800 2 92 00 49.

TIME

In Florida, the time zone is Eastern Standard Time (CET −6 hr), west of the Chattahoochee–Apalachicola line it is Central Standard Time (CET −7 h). Summer time is from March 2 to the first Sunday in November.

TIPPING

Waiters expect 15 to 20 per cent of the bill. Only in tourist centres is the gratuity/tip often already included in the price.

UNITS OF MEASUREMENT

1 mile = 1.61 km
1 gallon = 3.787 l
1 pound = 453.59 g
77 degrees Fahrenheit =
25 degrees Celsius
95 degrees Fahrenheit =
35 degrees Celsius
Ladies' sizes (clothing): 4 = 34; 6 = 36;
8 = 38; 10 = 40; 12 = 42 etc.
Gents' sizes: 36 = 46; 38 = 48;
40 =50 etc.

POST

Post offices are open Mon–Fri 8.30am–5pm, some also Sat 8.30am–noon. A letter or postcard to Europe costs $1.15

PRICES

As a rule, in the US prices are quoted without tax. So an additional 6% sales tax is payable, as well as a variable *tourist impact tax* in restaurants. So when looking at the menu or other prices, you will have to do a bit of calculating.

BUDGETING

Espresso	$4 /£3	
	in an independent café	
Wine	$13 /£10	
	per glass at Barton G.	
Snack	$11 /£8.50	
	chicken salad at a bistro	
T-shirt	$24 /£19	
	with the pink Florida flamingo	

BAHAMAS

In the turquoise waters on the Tropic of Cancer, more than 700 larger and more than 2000 smaller cayos or cays – tiny reef islands – lie scattered on the Great and Little Bahama Bank. Only 30 of the islands are inhabited and only 16 also have hotels and restaurants.

So it's an ideal region for Robinson Crusoe-type holiday-makers and water rats. Swimming, diving, snorkelling and sailing – for this the islands are ideally suited, and of course also for stopping over on a Caribbean cruise. Even the Bahamas' natural parks are mostly submarine, because the largely unspoilt coral world is the island's greatest attraction.

In 1973, after more than 300 years as an English colony, the Bahamas gained independence, although they remained a member of the British Commonwealth. Today the island state has a population of about 350,000. Of these, 85 per cent are descendants of the West African slaves imported by the plantation owners. Most Bahamans live on only two islands: New Providence, of which the capital is Nassau, and Grand Bahama. The other islands are only sparsely populated. Agriculture is hardly possible on the coral islands, and fishing and salt production provide work for only a few of the inhabitants. Consequently the state looks to tourism and international banking: almost 400 financial institutions in Nassau offer tax fugitives a safe haven.

Photo: The colourful houses are a characteristic feature of Nassau

"Baja mar", shallow sea, is what the Spanish conquerors called the island-speckled shelf banks between Florida and Cuba's southern tip.

NASSAU

(🗺 4/B2) **With a length of only 35 km, the island is not one of country's largest, but New Providence is the tourist hub of the Bahamas.**

This is where most of the holidaymakers go and where 70 per cent of the roughly 350,000 Bahamans live, most of them in the capital city of Nassau in the north-east. The other holiday destination is Paradise Island, a small off-shore island with palm-fringed beaches, resort hotels and a casino. The city's upswing started in 1940, when the Duke of Windsor, the abdicated English king, became governor-general of the Bahamas and elevated Nassau to the scandalous meeting place of the nobility and the moneyed aristocracy. Today megahotels, flourishing banks and a large cruise ship port result in much hustle and bustle. Join this lively scene as soon as your ship has moored and you have gone ashore!

SIGHTSEEING

OLD TOWN

The heart of Nassau's old city beats at the harbour, where the big cruise ships drop anchor at the Prince George Wharf. Nearby are Rawson Square and Parliament Square, seat of the Bahaman government, in the photogenic pink colonial buildings of 1805. There is a statue of the young Queen Victoria in front of the Parliament Building. Right in front of it runs Bay Street, the main arterial road of Nassau to the west: this is the city's business centre, with tax-free shops, eateries, jewellery stores and souvenir shops. On the colourful Straw Market, you can buy straw hats (hence the name), postcards and affordable arts and crafts (bargaining about the price is a tradition here). Following George Street towards the south, you pass the Christ Church Cathedral, built in 1841, and arrive at the imposing Government House (erected in 1801), residence of the English governor-general. The changing of the guard, as in London, takes place every second Saturday of the month with much pomp and circumstance.

FORT FINCASTLE ☀

A fort from 1787: from the 38 m high water tower, you get a great view of the city. Easily reached by the 66 steps of the Queen's Staircase. *Daily guided tours 8am–4pm | Admission B$1/US$1/£0.76*

JOHN WATLINGS DISTILLERY

On a free guided tour, you will learn everything about the Bahaman national drink. *Daily 10am–6 | 17 Delancy Street*

NATIONAL ART GALLERY

The works of Bahaman artists on display in a lovely old villa are often full of vibrant colour. In special exhibitions,

The statue of Christopher Columbus guards the Government Building

ON THE MENU AND ON THE STREET

They appear on every menu, their shells are used to pave streets, and they glitter seductively on souvenir stands: we're talking shells, those large, beautifully serrated marine snails found everywhere on the sandy beaches of the Bahaman coastlines. A conch (pronounced 'conk') takes 4 years to reach maturity; older shells can weigh up to 3 kg and reach a length of 40 cm. The female produces up to 1 million eggs, but this hardly satisfies the ravenous Bahamans. The flesh is served soaked in lemon juice and pungent chillies (scorched conch), tenderised and deep fried (cracked conch), as chowder or as a salad. But no matter how bright they are, they are no good as souvenirs – in other countries the conch is deemed a threatened species and therefore falls under the Washington Convention for the protection of species and may not be exported.

the Junkanoo carnival costumes are usually also displayed. *Tue–Sat 10am–5pm, Sun noon–5pm | Admission B$7/ US$/£5.33 | West Street/West Hill Street | nagb.org.bs*

PARADISE ISLAND
The 5 km/3 mi long island combines everything that goes into the perfect holiday cocktail: shopping malls, a casino with extravagant shows, a golf course, crystal-clear water and a dream beach with powdery sand along the whole northern coast of the island. *Bridge to Nassau | Toll B$2/£1.5*

POMPEY MUSEUM
On the old slave market of 1769 the history of slavery on the Bahamas is retold. *Mon–Sat 9.30am–4.30, Thu till 1pm; temporarily closed for renovation | Admission B$3/£2.30 West Bay Street/ George Street/www.ammcbahamas.com*

SEAWORLD EXPLORER
An underwater trip for hydrophobes: take a submarine to view the corals and colourful fish. *Ticket B$49/£37.40*

| Departure from the Straw Market in the cruise port | Tel. 3 56 25 48 | www.bahamas.com/vendor/seaworld-explorer

FOOD & DRINK

CAFÉ MATISSE
A popular bistro in the Old Town quarter. Italian cuisine, great for lunch in the idyllic courtyard. *Tel. 3 56 70 12 46 | Moderate).*

GOLDIE'S CONCH HOUSE
In this Bahaman fast food hut you can watch how the conchs are prepared. Served with fish and cold beer. *Arawak Cay | Tel. 3 25 43 00 | Budget*

GRAYCLIFF
This gourmet restaurant is stylishly located in a splendid colonial villa. Caribbean cuisine with a dash of French inspiration, besides which this establishment has the best cellar of all the Bahamas. Jackets are obligatory. *West Hill Street/ Blue Hill Road | Tel. 3 02 91 50 | www. graycliff. com | Expensive*

The "swimming pigs" of Big Major

SHOPPING

From original T-shirts to perfume and luxury watches: if you cannot find it on Bay Street and on the Straw Market, you won't find it anywhere on the Bahamas.

LEISURE & SPORT

DOLPHIN ENCOUNTERS

How about redefining your cruise stopover a little differently? Here's a special

TRAVEL WITH KIDS

Look up Captain Blackbeard and his ship's crew on his ship, the Revenge: the excellently designed multimedia museum *Pirates of Nassau* resurrects the world of the freebooters. *Mon–Sat 9am–6pm, Sun 9am–noon | Admission B$13/£10, children under 17 years 6.50 B$/£5 | Marlborough/ George Street | Nassau | Bahamas | www. piratesofnassau.com.*

and definitely unforgettable tip: swimming with dolphins and sea lions in a naturally shaped lagoon on an offshore island. B$109–350/£83–267. *Departure from ferry office of the Paradise Island bridge | Nassau | Tel. 3 63 10 03 | www. dolphinencounters.com*

WHERE TO GO

EXUMAS ★

If you have enough time on your cruise, you should not pass up this experience: on a day trip to the uninhabited islands of the northern Exumas you experience the most delightful side of the Bahamas: in a power boat you race across the turquoise waters. During the breaks you can go snorkelling, swim and watch iguanas. *Powerboat Adventures | approx. B$200/£153 | Tel. 3 63 22 65 | www. powerboatadventures.com*

From George Town (pop. 1500) on Great Exuma, a popular boat trip takes you to **INSIDER TIP** Big Major, where the now famous "swimming pigs" live – feral domestic pigs with a passion for water *(Day trip approx. 180 B$/£187.50 | www. exumawater tours.com).*

SAN SALVADOR (*m 4/C3*)

So this is it, Columbus's island of Guanahani, where Cristobal Colón first set foot on the soil of the New World in 1492. Although historians disagree, the lagoons in the interior of the island, which is barely 10 km long, seem to confirm the log that Columbus kept. The most important of the no less than 4 monuments to Columbus, a large white cross, stands on the beach about 5 km south of the island's only city, Cockburn Town. On the northern tip of the island is the ☀ Dixon Hill Lighthouse, which has been running on paraffin since it was built in 1856.

TRAVEL TIPS

 Bahamas: the most important information for your trip

BERTH

Cruise ships dock in the Prince George Dock of Nassau's port. The Prince George Dock is near the city centre; you can reach downtown Nassau on foot in about fifteen minutes.

EMERGENCY SERVICES

The emergency numbers on the Bahamas are 911 and 919. Nassau and Grand Bahama have proper hospitals with specialty practitioners. Ambulances are only available on New Providence and Grand Bahama.

HEALTH

Taking out international health insurance is recommended. Drink only boiled or bottled water. That way you avoid risking infections.

IMMIGRATION

To enter the Bahamas, you need a passport that is still valid for six months. If you enter via the US on your cruise, a machine-readable pass is required; newly issued passes must contain biometric data.

INTERNETCAFÉS & WIFI

On the Bahamas, web cafés and hotspots can only be found in Nassau and Freeport. WiFi and internet kiosks in the Welcome Center of the *Festival Place | Prince George Wharf | Nassau*

MONEY & CREDIT CARDS

Restaurants and shops accept Master and Visa cards. You can draw money at ATMs with the EC card – that's less expensive than with a credit card.

PRICES & CURRENCY

The home currency of the Bahamas is the Bahaman dollar (B$). It is linked 1:1 to the US dollar. US dollars are also accepted as a means of payment. You can also pay with common credit cards.

TRAVELLING BY BUS

There are inexpensive Jitney buses running in Nassau. A single trip costs about B$1/£0,73. The buses run frequently and you can explore the whole island by bus.

BUDGETING

Restaurant	B$20/£15.30
	Three-Course menu in a mid-range restaurant
Water	B$1.50/£1.10
	1 glass (0.33 l)
Local traffic	B$1.30/£1
	Single ticket

TURKS AND CAICOS ISLANDS

The Turks and Caicos Islands, which have exactly 40 rainy days a year, are – completely unjustifiably – overshadowed by the neighbouring Dominican Republic.

These islands lie in the north-western part of the archipelago, and most of the inhabitants live on the island called Providence. The Turks Islands in the south-west are distinctly smaller; the main island is Grand Turk and the capital is Cockburn Town. They are a proud people – proud of belonging to the British Crown, because the Turks and Caicos Islands are a British Overseas Territory, and Queen Elisabeth II is locally represented by a governor. And, of course, proud of their breathtaking nature: the sea, which invites you to indulge in any and all forms of water sport, the dream beaches, the special plant and animal world, such as the Turks and Caicos rock iguana, which is found nowhere else, and numerous submarine cave systems. And not least of the fact that after orbiting around the earth in an Atlas rocket in 1962, the American astronaut John Glenn put his feet on the soil of Grand Turk first.

GRAND TURK ISLAND

It was salt that brought the first British settlers here – colonists that arrived from Bermuda in 1681. However, they were not the first inhabit-

A real Caribbean dream: 100 islands, turquoise seas and a radiant blue sky that seems to go on forever

ants of Grand Turk Island; long before them the Taíno lived here, having probably drifted here around 700 BC from the south and dying out in the early 15th century.

The new inhabitants laid out salt pans on the island, which – especially in the beginning of the 20th century – did very well. When the salt pans went into a decline after the 1950s because of low production volumes, many of the colonial buildings from the time of the second colonisation remained; they have been especially well preserved on *Duke* and *Front Street* in Cockburn Town, the capital of the Turks and Caicos Islands since 1766. But there are also the remains of the former salt pans; for example, those of the salt works *Hawkes Nest* near the cruise ship terminal. The free-ranging donkeys are yet another leftover from the production of the white gold; they are the descendants of the animals that were put to work in the salt works, and you just might run into them when you disembark.

SIGHTSEEING

GRAND TURK LIGHTHOUSE
Curiously, the lighthouse (built in 1852) is the only lighthouse on all of the Turks and Caicos Islands. It no longer fulfils its former purpose of safely guiding ships past the northern coast of Grand Turk, but with its bright white paint it is a conspicuous beacon in front of the shining blue sea. The area around the lighthouse can be visited for a fee. There is a picturesque footpath from the lighthouse along the shore. *Open daily | Admission US$3/£2.30 | Lighthouse Road*

HER MAJESTY'S PRISON
The prison, built in the early 19th century and enlarged over the years (and the only one on the entire archipelago) with its bell tower, the ringing of which used to mark the start and end of the inmates' working hours, remained in use until 1994 and is now open to the public. *Open when cruise ships are moored in port | Admission US$7/£5.30 | Pond Street, Cockburn Town*

THE SALT HOUSE
The small museum and adjacent café and souvenir shop offer visitors a view of the island's formerly most important

economic driver, the production of salt. There is, among others, an exhibition of the so-called *Bermuda sloops,* boats that were used to transport salt. Other things to see: salt channels and a functional windmill. *Open when cruise ships are moored in port | Free admission | Osborne Rd, Cockburn Town*

NICELY CALCIFIED

The Turks and Caicos Islands consist mainly of limestone, which is the main rock type on all islands and is seen everywhere on all the islands. The weatherability of limestone manifests itself in numerous ways. Especially noteworthy is the process of karstification, which is demonstrated especially by the formation of caves and the *blue holes*. Most impressive are the Ocean Hole on Middle Caicos and the Conch Bar Caves, a huge system of caves, also on Middle Caicos.

Almost like in paradise: lonely beaches and the endless sea under blue skies on Middle Caicos

TURKS AND CAICOS NATIONAL MUSEUM

What could be more fitting than that a museum of insular history is housed on the historic *Front Street* in Cockburn Town in *Guinep House*, one of the oldest buildings on the island? The museum, opened in 1991, is dedicated especially to the *Molasses Reef Wreck*, the wreck of a Spanish or Portuguese caravel of the 16th century that ran aground on the reef off Provenciales and sank. The *Taíno*, the ancient first inhabitants of the island, are another focus of the exhibition. *Varying opening hours (information at www. tcmuseum.org, Rubrik Tours) | Admission US$5/£3.80 | Guinep House, Front Street, Cockburn*

WHALE WATCHING ★

In the winter months, you have the opportunity to watch humpback whales off Grand Turk when they pass the islands on their trek from the North Atlantic to the Caribbean. The *Humpback Dive Shack* offers a special experience: swimming eye to eye with a humpback whale! The operator emphasises considerate interaction with the animals and neither harasses nor chases them. The tours take place from January to April, usually from 9am to 1pm. Special times can be arranged for cruise ship tourists to fit the berthing schedule, as well as transfer to and from the ship. *US$140/£107 | Close Haul Road | www.humpbackdiveshack.com*

FOOD & DRINK

SANDBAR RESTAURANT ♨

Eating and drinking with a view – and what a view! The name already says it: the Sand Bar lies right on the water

TRAVEL WITH KIDS

Would you like to do more with your children than spend a day on the beach with them, and make them more familiar with the exciting world of birds on Grand Turk? The best way is to rent a car (can also be done at the Grand Turk Cruise Center) and head for the best birdwatching sites on the small island. That would be, among others, the salt pans, North Wells and South Wells as well as the South Creek and North Creek mangrove marshes. Here you can see flamingos and herons, for example. You can order the PDF brochure *"Birding in Paradise"* on the website of the UK Overseas Territories Conservation Forum *(www.ukotcf. org, tab Territories & Tours)* . This brochure guides you to the best birding sites on the island.

and offers an incomparable view of the sea – and if your luck is in and you are in the right place at the right time, of the passing whales as well. On the menu you will find fresh shellfish *(conch)*, and the rum-based cocktails are recommended. *Manta House | Duke Street | Tel. 649 243-2666|www.grandturk-mantahouse.com/ sandbar.htm*

A maritime highlight on the Gibb's Cay beach

TURKS HEAD INNE

The very finest of colonial Caribbean backdrops, and loaded with history to boot: the building was erected around 1830 and was used among others as the guest house of the British governor and as an American consulate. Specialities of the restaurant in the boutique hotel are the pizzas and the house ice cream. *Cockburn Town | Tel. 1 649 946 1830 | www.turksheadinne. com*

WHERE TO GO

INSIDER TIP ▶ GIBB'S CAY

This islet lies about 1 km/1 mi off the eastern coast of Grand Turk and boast not only a fantastic beach, but also a rare natural phenomenon: the numerous stingrays that gather when boats turn up. Anyone who has ever wanted to watch these unique, majestic animals swimming in their natural habitat should not miss this opportunity. For cruise ship passengers, special excursions to Gibbs Cay are offered from the cruise ship terminal; other excursions start from the capital Cockburn Town.

TRAVEL TIPS

 Turks and Caicos: the most important information for your trip

BEACHES

Access to the beaches on the Turks and Caicos Islands is free; there are no private beaches.

BERTH

At Grand Turk Island, cruise ships moor at the southern end of the island. In fact, the Grand Turk port is the only one of the archipelagos where cruise ships dock. The island's Grand Turk Cruise Center of more than 50,000 m²/5 ha has shops, a Margaritaville restaurant and a large swimming pool. There is also the Cruise Center Beach, where cruise ship passengers can spend their time if they do not plan to explore the island.

HEALTH

There are hospitals on the islands of Providenciales and Grand Turk. An international health insurance policy is recommended. In the rainy season, from April to July, precautions should be taken against mosquitoes. Poisonwood can cause a rash on contact. Its yellow fruit is highly toxic.

LANGUAGE

The official language on the Turks and Caicos Islands is English.

MOBILE PHONE & INTERNET

On the Turks and Caicos islands you can use mobile phones which are compatible with the GSM or the CDMA standard. The mobile phone companies Digicell and Flow operate on the islands. For frequent telephone calls, a SIM card of the local network operators may be advisable. The 4G telephony standard is used on the islands. WiFi is available in many cafés and restaurants. Country code for Turks and Caicos Islands: *+1 649.*

MONEY & CREDIT CARDS

On the Turks and Caicos islands, all payments are made in US dollars. The usual credit cards are accepted in many shops and restaurants.

TRANSPORT

There is no public local transport on Grand Turk. If you want to explore the island on your own, you therefore have to make use of rental cars and taxis, which can also be booked at the cruise ship terminal.

BUDGETING

Cappuccino	US$6/£4.60
	1 cup
Lunch	US$20/£15.25
	with drink

GREATER ANTILLES

Everlasting sun, waters that shimmer in blue and green, powdery white beaches, hillsides planted with sugar cane and dense rainforests – these are common to all the larger islands of the northern Caribbean.

But of course it is not only nature and climate that make the islands of the Greater Antilles so special. It's also the people living here, this colourful mixture of ancient inhabitants, descendants of the former slaves and colonial masters and all the other immigrants from all over the world. Most of the islands are not large, so people who originally came from diverse cultures had to adjust to each other – at least as regards language: the Chinese dealer speaks the same Patois, the

melodic language of Jamaica, as the DJ shaking his dreadlocks or the Indian nurse. Many Muslims go to church if there is no mosque: one religion is as good as another. And on the English-speaking islands you often encounter an upbeat religiousness. The pastor's threatening harangues alternate with cheerful gospel singing by the congregation – more like a party than respectful devotion. The constant breeze of the trade winds keeps the subtropical climate at a pleasant 28–29 °C. This is probably what has made the love of life of the people of all Caribbean nations so legendary: in all life situations they dance, make music, laugh and celebrate with a will.

History and culture on the islands are as diverse as nature above and below water – immerse yourself in a different world.

CUBA

Let's say this right at the outset: nothing much has changed on Cuba yet. It is still the only communist country in the West, the economic blockade by the USA is still in place (although it has loosened up a bit); the revolutionaries of yore are still there, and the country is still poor – despite the numerous economic reforms introduced by president Raúl Castro, who has allowed the establishment of small businesses and entrepreneurship.

Cuba has always been "special", first to Columbus, who enthused about the beauty of the island, and then to the conquerors of Latin America, who chose Cuba as the port where they gathered and headed back to Spain with their treasure-laden galleons. Later the Spanish island, still ruled by Spain, could boast that it was the world's largest producer of sugar. It became a complete legend, however, through the revolution, when bearded men in battle dress – headed by Fidel Castro and his brother Raúl, Camilo Cienfuegos and the Argentinian Ernesto "Che" Guevara – drove the dictator Fulgencio Batista from the island to establish a more just society.

HAVANNA

"In Havana, my friend, everything is possible if you're no slouch." That's how the locals describe life in the Cuban metropolis.

This sentiment has never been more apt than now, when a multifaceted small-business sector is showing the ponderous socialist state apparatus what can be done. The streets are fringed by small snack bars, bicycle taxis offer their services, as do private taxis – all of it at Cuban peso prices for Cubans and at the correct CUC (Cuban Convertible Peso) exchange rate for tourists. It all looks a bit like a secret takeover of Havana by its citizens or by the spirit of free enterprise.

SIGHTSEEING

INSIDER TIP ▶ CALLEJÓN DE HAMEL (🗺 6/A2)

The murals in the alley, the small Santería shop filled with cult objects and the corner café alone are already worth a visit. Every Sunday *(noon–5pm)* there's an exuberant street party here (now irregularly, alas): groups beat the drums for all they're worth and men and women dance themselves into a trance on the open street. *Callejón de Hamel | between Aramburu/Hospital Street*

LA HABANA VIEJA ★ (🗺 6/C–D2)

Alley after alley, square after square

Historical façades with the Capitol in the background

CAUTION – BEARERS OF SECRETS!

Ever seen a Cuban dressed all in white? Completely in white, from shoes and socks to scarf? He's "studying to come a saint" (hacerse santo), they say. Only Cubans who want to be ordained as a Babalawo dress in this way. A Babalawo is a priest of Santeria, an Afro-Cuban religion that arose out of the cultural clash of Christianity and African Yoruba beliefs brought to the Americas by slaves. Their dress indicates that they carry secrets: for a year they are initiated into the rituals, songs and stories of Santería. On Cuba, this is the most widely spread religion. It holds that at least one god from the Santería pantheon can be assigned to any person: perhaps Ochún, the goddes of vanity, Oyá, the goddes of revenge, Yemayá, the goddess of the sea and of motherhood, or Ogún, the heroine, warrior and god of the mountains. Would you like to know which god suits you? Ask a Babalawo!

decorated with beautiful buildings from various periods – and music everywhere: *La Habana Vieja*, the Old Town, is not a Unesco World Heritage site for nothing, a monument bursting with life to the centuries-long, almost uninterrupted rise of a city that once was one of America's richest. Each era left its mark. A small temple *(El Templete)* on the *Plaza de Armas* recalls 1591 when the *Villa San Cristóbal de la Habana*, built five years earlier by Diego Velázquez, was moved to its present place; the first fortifications, such as the Castillo de Real Fuerza, testify to its promotion (1535) to the gathering point of all Spanish treasure vessels from Central and South America. That there were riches to defend is borne out by the remains of the old city walls and isolated bulwarks, but particularly by the gigantic fortified complex of *Morro-Cabaña*. Every step of the way you find witnesses of Cuba's times as the world's biggest supplier of sugar: opulent palaces with wooden balconies, lordly entrances or high wooden doors with ornate *aldabas* (knockers). Hotels, restaurants and bars moved into the restored buildings, while the *Avenida del Puerto* at the old port morphed into a neat avenue with cruise ship and ferry berths. The *Parque Central*, the Capitol and the old *Barrio Chino* are already part of *Habana Centro*, which with the lively *Calles Galiano* and *Rafael* has its own business streets, and at the *Malecón* it can be seen from its best side.

MUSEO DE LA REVOLUCIÓN (🏛 O/C1)

Interest in this museum in the former presidential palace of 1920 has never been greater than now! The queue of visitors, many of whom are Americans, often stretches back from the entrance to the relic of the old city wall. In the entry hall, homage is paid to the *chefe en comandante* Fidel Castro, who died in 2016; his fellow-combatants Che Guevara and Camilo Cienfuegos then "jump" at you farther up, where the chronological tour starts, in the form of life-size wax effigies in guerilla dress. An entrance takes you to the display space with the yacht Granma, in which the rebels landed on the eastern side of Cuba in 1956. *Refugio 1 | between Monserrate/ Zulueta | Daily 9.30am–4pm| Admission CUC8/£6.1, guided tour CUC2/£1.53*

MUSEO NACIONAL DE BELLAS ARTES *(📖 6/C2)*

The National Museum of Fine Arts is accommodated in two separate buildings: pearls of Cuban painting from the different centuries are displayed in the modern building on the Calle Trocadero *(between Zulueta/Montserrate)*; the collection of international art in the former Centro Asturiano *(C/ San Rafael | between Zulueta/Montserrate)*, which was built in the style of the Parisian opera house in 1928. *Both Tue–Sat 9am–5pm, Sun 10am–2pm | Admission CUC8/£6.13, single CUC5/£3.82 each | www.bellasartes.co.cu*

PARQUE CENTRAL/PRADO *(📖 6/C2)*

Karl Lagerfeld knew very well why he had his 2016 models strut their stuff on the *Paseo de Martí*, or Prado for short, with his Chanel collection. The promenade, guarded by lion sculptures and romantically lit up by old brass lanterns, resembles a red carpet for Havana's golden centre. The promenade leads to the *Parque Central*, which covers several city blocks. This is where the open hop-on-hop-off buses stop *(CUC10/£7.66 per day, various stops)*, and here highly polished oldtimers *(CUC50/£38.30 1 h)* and horse-drawn carriages *(1 h round trip for 4 persons CUC40/£30.65)* are waiting for fares. You get a good view of the hustle and bustle in the park from the boulevard café of the nostalgic hotel Inglaterra (Tel. 78 60 85 93 | 78 60 85 97 | www. hotel inglaterra-cuba.com). The adjacent building is worth a special visit: the restored *Gran Teatro de La Habana Alicia Alonso*, in which Enrico Caruso sang. But as ever, the park is dominated by the Capitol, which in 1929 unashamedly copied the White House in Washington. Since 2018, this has been the seat of the Cuban parliament. This way, parliament has the (Afro-Cuban) gods right beside them: on the *Paseo del Prado no. 615 in the Museo de los Orishas (daily 9am–4pm| Admission CUC5/£7.66)*. There is also a shadow from the past: the Barrio Chino with its Chinese gate. Thousands of Chinese used to live here, enticed by false promises after the slaves had been freed. The few who stayed behind are spreading a bit of Asian flair in the Calle Cuchillo.

PLAZA DE ARMAS *(📖 6/D2)*

The city's oldest square. Trees dispense shade, benches invite you to tarry, and the noise-absorbing wooden planks laid in front of the former *Palacio de los Capitanes Generales (Tue–Sun 9.30am–5pm | Admission CUC3/£2.30)* remind people to be quiet – if there doesn't happen to be a concert being performed on them. In the patio of the former seat and residence of Cuba's captains-general (1791), a statue of Cuba's discoverer Columbus bids you welcome; inside, the city's history is unfolded. The palace of the Duke of Santevenia opposite is hardly more modest; today it is home to the Hotel Santa Isabel.

TRAVEL WITH KIDS

Aparatos from China such as the *Montaña Rusa* (roller coaster), swings, slides and many more in the play and amusement park *Isla del Coco* in the capital city offer great fun and opportunities for intercultural encounters across all language barriers. *5a Av./C/ 112 | Miramar | Wed–Sun 10am–6pm| Admission 1 Peso/£0.76*

A place of rest and meditation in Havana: the Plaza de Armas

The chapel El Templete (1828) on the left is quite unprepossessing by comparison! Yet it stands on very significant historical soil, namely the spot where in 1519 the foundation mass for la Villa San Cristóbal de La Habana was said. At the time, the neighbouring Castillo de la Real Fuerza, now Havana's oldest fortress (1577), was the first-line defence against attacks. Can you see the small figure on the fortress? That is the Giradilla, the symbol of Havana! It represents Ines de Bobadilla, looking out in vain for her husband, the Cuban governor Hernando de Soto – not knowing that he had died of fever on the Mississippi. You can see the original of this oldest forging made in Havana (1630) at the entrance to the INSIDER TIP *Museo de Navegación (Tue–Sun 9.30am–5pm| Admission CUC3/£2.30)*. Inside, some large model ships take you back to Havana's

early years, when it was the first royal shipyard of New Spain.

PLAZA VIEJA (*6/D2*)

The square where there is always something going on – as if it were still the main market and trading place, which it was in the mid-16th century. The stateliest house, decorated with a wrought-iron balcony, is the Casa del Conde de Jaruco (1768). In the corner building Gómez Vila (1909) there is a *cámara oscura (daily 9am–6pm | admission CUC2/£1.53)* that projects a panorama of the surroundings in real time. There's good eating at the *Taberna La Muralla (daily | Cnr C/ La Muralla | Budget/Moderate)*, and in the evening people meet in the *Café el Escorial (daily 9am–9pm| Budget/Moderate)*. In the nearby *Calle Oficios 254/ Muralla (towards the port)* Cuba's 'second discoverer'

CUBA

is honoured in the *Casa Alejandro Humboldt (Tue–Sun 9am–5pm| free admission);* Alexander von Humboldt explored Cuba in 1800 and 1801.

CITY WALL/MUSEO CASA NATAL DE JOSÉ MARTÍ *(🗺 6/C3)*
Railway neighbourhoods are often regarded as dubious; this also applies to those of Havana around the *Calle Paula.* This is

LOCAL SPECIALITIES

CULT DRINKS MADE IN CUBA
A lime, six fresh mint leaves, a teaspoon of sugar, two centilitres of rum, soda water, a sprig of mint – there you have Cuba's national drink, the mojito. Or how about a soft green daiquiri with cane syrup, rum and lime juice, the way the great Ernest Hemingway is said to have loved it? Or a Mary Pickford, a Havana special, a canchanchara and, last but not least, a Cuba libre? Whether it's a Cuba libre, mojito or daiquiri: for mixing you use white rum that has matured in oak barrels for at least five years. When it's older, it turns darker and is called añejo.

where Cuba's liberation hero and author José Martí grew up. The house of his birth, the Casa Natal de José Martí *(C/ Leonor Pérez 314 | Tue–Sat 9am–5pm | Admission CUC2/£1.53)*, is opposite the station. In between: remains of the old city wall!

FOOD & DRINK

INSIDER TIP O'REILLY 304 *(🗺 6/C2)*
Trendy hangout for taco aficionados and friends of fresh (seafood) cuisine like ceviche (marinated raw fish/seafood). Good cocktails. *Daily noon–midnight | C/O'Reilly 304/betw. Habana/Aguiar | Tel. 0 52 64 47 25 | Budget–Moderate*

CASTILLO DE FARNÉS *(🗺 6/C2)*
The waiter will be happy to point out the table at which Fidel Castro, his brother Raúl and Che Guevara ate on 9.1.1959. There's a photo to recall the event. The food is good and inexpensive. *Daily noon–midnight | Av. Monserrate 401 | Cnr Obrapía | Tel. 78 67 10 30 | Moderate*

INSIDER TIP IIVAN CHEF JUSTO *(🗺 6/C1)*
Private restaurant of a top chef. Shellfish or calabash cream – Ivan's hors d'oeuvres are real poetry. *Daily noon–midnight | Aguacate 9 | Cnr Chacón | Tel. 78 63 96 97 | Mobile 0 53 43 85 40 | Moderate–Expensive*

SHOPPING

CALLE AGUÍAR ("SCISSORS ALLEY") *(🗺 6/C1)*
A gigantic pair of scissors before the tiny pedestrian zone points the way to Havana's most famous barber. On the top floor of no. 10 Calle Aguíar, Gilberto Valladares, Papito for short, practises his blend of barbershop and museum, which he calls *Arte Corte (Mon–Sat noon–6pm).* Every piece tells a story, even the chair on

SPOIL YOURSELF

Who, when thinking of Cuba, does not also think of those famous cigars, the havanas? Sure, smoking puts your health at risk, but anyone who appreciates cigars should indulge themselves and take along at least a small stock from the country of origin. The best opportunity to buy genuine havanas is to visit the cigar factories (fábricas de tabaco), where you are allowed to watch the tabaqueros at work. A novel experience: when readers entertain the workers with stories! Be careful when cigars are offered in the street! They are almost always imitations of the well-known brands such as Cohiba, Romeo y Julieta or Montecristo. Remember: to export more than 50 cigars you must present the seller's proof of sale (original and copy for Customs); furthermore, the cigars must be in their original packaging and bear the new holographic stamp.

which you have your hair cut. If you stroll past the restaurants, you will see *Pedro's (no. 17)* basement boutique on your left, which specialises in elegant and discrete leisure wear. *Between C / Peña Pobre*

INSIDER TIP MUSEO DEL CHOCOLATE *(𝄒 6/D2)*
With a bit of luck, you can watch the preparation of the delicious chocolates before you buy them. Or have a mug of the good cacao from Baracoa – tasty, whether warm or cold! *C/Mercaderes 255 / Chi Amargura*

WHERE TO GO

MATANZAS *(𝄒 5/B1)*
If the duration of your stay in Cuba permits, a visit to Matanzas is recommended. This city, located on a bay on the northern coast approximately 160 km to the east of Havana, has a population of about 150,000. The large number of 17th century houses in the Spanish style give Matanzas an almost nostalgic appearance. The town is worth visiting mainly because of its caves, the **INSIDER TIP** *Cuevas de Bellamar (daily*

9am–5pm | Guided tour CUC8/£6.2). Rock paintings prove that people already lived here 1600 years ago. You can explore part of the subterranean cave system on foot.

MUSEO HEMINGWAY ★ *(𝄒 5/B1)*
Hemingway occupied the villa until shortly before his death in 1961. His furniture, books, trophies and writing tools are still in the same place. *Mon–Sat 10am–5pm, Sun 10am–1pm | Admission CUC5/£3.82 | San Francisco de Paula | appr. 17 km southeast of Havana*

BERTH

In Havana, cruise ships moor at the Terminal Sierra Maestra, near the Plaza de San Francisco de Asis in the Old Town of the Cuban capital. The historical centre can be reached on foot from the cruise ship terminal, which is to be greatly extended by 2024.

CAYMAN ISLANDS

The Cayman Islands lie in the middle of the Caribbean Sea, about 200 km south-east of Cuba and a little farther north-west of Jamaica.

The total population of the three islands is just 49,000, of which a relatively large proportion (almost 40 per cent) are foreigners who have settled here. Not only for that reason, but also because of the flourishing offshore banking business (the Cayman Islands are a tax paradise) and the international tourism industry, the islands are very prosperous. Tourists are drawn especially by the kilometres of beaches and the outstanding diving sites.

GRAND CAYMAN

(☒ 5/B–C3) **The largest of the three islands is a little more than 30 km/18.5 mi long and 6 km/3,7 mi wide. Georgetown, the capital of the British crown colony, is on this island.**

TRAVEL WITH KIDS

Would you like to give your children a sense of 'Pirates of the Caribbean'? One can go hunting for traces in the former pirate caves, where the freebooters used to hide their booty. For animal and nature lovers, there is also a petting zoo with an educational trail. *Daily 9am–6pm | Admission US$8/£6.12, children between 4 and 12 years US$5/£3.83 | 277 Bodden Town Rd | www.piratescaves.ky*

International banks, attracted by the favourable banking environment, have branches here. Most of Grand Cayman consists of marshland; human settlements are limited to the west, the north-west and the coast.

SIGHTSEEING

ATLANTIS SUBMARINE ⭐
Several times a day the little submarine takes groups of curious people closer to the marvels of the coral reefs without having to resort to diving equipment. The panoramic window gives an excellent view of the plant and animal life on the reef. Book early! *Daily | from US$94/£37.5 | Waterfront | Georgetown | Tel. 9 49 77 00 | www.caymanislandssubmarines.com*

CAYMAN ISLANDS NATIONAL MUSEUM
The museum in the erstwhile courthouse gives an insight into the pirate history of the islands. *Mon–Fri 9am–5pm, Sat 10am–2pm | Admission US$8/£6.12 | Waterfront | Georgetown*

CAYMAN TURTLE CENTRE
The main reason why pirates and other seafarers kept coming to the islands was the turtles – their meat and eggs were a welcome supplement to the monotonous shipboard diet. The stock of turtles has dwindled substantially; many of the beaches they visit to lay their eggs have fallen into human hands since. The turtle farm returns a certain part of the animals bred here to the sea, thus contributing to the preservation of the species. Nevertheless, it should not be overlooked that it is primarily a commercial enterprise that supplies input material for culinary delicacies and fashion accessories. The Cayman

In the Cayman Turtle Centre, you can get close to the turtles, which are so graceful under water

Turtle Centre is approx. 14 km/8.5 mi north of Georgetown. *Daily 8am–5pm | US$18–45/£13.8–34.4 | Boatswain's Beach | Northwest Point | West Bay | Tel. 9 49 38 94 | www.turtle.ky*

GEORGETOWN

The small town has 27,000 residents and is a lively economic hub. Not only do the banks have their branches in Georgetown; there are also many shops that have maritime offers, in particular for holidaymakers.

HELL

Would you like to send your loved ones back home a nice little postcard about your cruise experience straight from Hell? No problem; the town, which owes its popularity with the English-speaking tourists mainly to its name, is geared to such intentions. Besides the card, you also get the appropriate stamp. *Approx. 12 km/7.5 mi north of Georgetown*

PEDRO ST JAMES

The oldest building on Grand Cayman *(approx. 12 km/7.5 mi south-east of Georgetown)* is said to have been built by a Spanish settler called Pedro Gomez in 1635. However, it was probably built only in 1780 as the fortified property of an Englishman. 'Pedro's castle' burnt down twice before it was restored to its present state and declared a national monument. *Daily 9am–5pm | Admission US$10/£7.65 | Old Jones Bay, East End, on the coastal South Sound Road | pedrostjames.ky*

QUEEN ELIZABETH II BOTANIC PARK

The whole exuberantly colourful spectacle of Caribbean nature is waiting for you in this beautifully laid out park

BERTH

Cruise ships head for the island's capital Georgetown on Grand Cayman. The ships do not moor in port; they anchor offshore and tender boats take the passengers ashore. The transfer takes about 15 minutes. Georgetown has three cruise terminals: the Watler Cruise Terminal, the North Terminal and the South Terminal. All three lie close together and in the immediate vicinity of the town centre, which you can easily reach on foot. If you are planning an excursion outside Georgetown, you will find taxis at the Royal Watler Terminal. Minibuses depart from the Edward Street stop.

with different sections, such as the Heritage Garden, which focuses on life on the Cayman Islands in the early 20th century, or you can marvel at the rare blue iguanas. *Daily 9.30am–5.30pm (last admission 4.30pm) | Admission US$12/£9.20 | North Side | www. botanic-park.ky*

STINGRAY CITY
Are you stopping over long enough and would like to explore the fascinating underwater world of the Cayman Islands yourself? Stingray City offer you the ideal options. Here in the North Sound you can go swimming in the company of tame stingrays. With their extremely wide fins, these large, beautiful fish glide over the sea floor like flying carpets. Visit *Stingray City Tour Operator (US$49–62/£37.5–47.5 | Tel.*

3453223400 | www.stingraycitycaymanislands.com).

SHOPPING

In Georgetown you will find a range of shops specialising in porcelain, jewellery, old gold and silver coins, duty-free perfume as well as spirits. Behind the Seven Mile Beach there are also a number of American-style shopping plazas.

ARTIFACTS LTD.
Here you find the best **INSIDER TIP** 'pirate coins', finds from sunken ships, guaranteed genuine with a certificate – but not exactly cheap! *Harbour Drive | Waterfront | Georgetown | Tel. 9 49 24 42*

FOOD & DRINK

LUCA
Italian-Cayman cuisine in a stylish beach restaurant. The fresh red snapper with lemon risotto and asparagus-and-almond salad is out of this world! Fresh pasta delights and outstanding wine list. Book your visit! *Tue–Sun | Caribbean Club | Seven Mile Beach | 871 West Bay Road | Tel. 34 56 23 45 50 | Expensive*

REEF GRILL
Cayman cuisine and live entertainment under the stars. On the veranda, which is framed by small palms, it's a little more laid back than in the posh inside rooms. *Royal Palms Beach Club | Tel. 9 45 63 58 | Moderate–Expensive*

BEACHES

If during your cruise you simply want to enjoy some Caribbean beach feeling, no problem. On the northern side of the island, there's Rum Point, where – if you are on the Cayman Islands during the weekend – you can also enjoy a barbecue and live music at the *Rum Point Club*. Grand Cayman's showcase beach is *Seven Mile Beach*, only about 5 km/3.1 mi north of Georgetown, with fine sand and fringed with Australian pines. There are also bars, restaurants and numerous water sports providers.

JAMAICA

(🕮 5/D–E4) **The Indian name Xaymaca can be translated as 'country of forests and waters'. With this name the original inhabitants, the Arawaks, captured the diversity of the island's nature in rather modest terms.**

Jamaica is the island of mountains and waterfalls, tropical forests, white, palm-fringed beaches, turquoise swimming coves and sugar-cane fields. The Jamaicans (around 2.8 million) are descendants of a variety of peoples, including – besides the descendants of African slaves – Indians, Chinese and Arabs as well as other Europeans. All of their languages influenced the Jamaican patois, which is also the basis of reggae and calypso texts. Most Jamaicans are friendly and have a great sense of humour.

MONTEGO BAY

(🕮 5/D4) **Jamaica's second largest city (pop. 100,000) has always been the centre of the northern coast.**

The products of the nearby plantations were shipped from here, and this is where the luxury goods the planters did not want to do without arrived from Europe. Downtown, the busy centre of the metropolis of about 100,000 residents, is a mixture of old and new –

with modern concrete houses and simple wooden shacks, congested streets, numerous small shops and even more street vendors.

Hardly any historic edifices are left in the city centre – raging fires in 1795 and 1811 destroyed them.

Casually Caribbean: Doctor's Cave beach

MONTEGO BAY CULTURAL CENTRE
Large-scale abstract paintings, flashy and mystic links to Caribbean colorimetry. Busts whose design is not really decoded by the title: with its varying exhibitions, the cultural centre aims to be artistic avant-garde and mirror the contemporary art scene at the same time. To this end there is a small permanent exhibition on the Rasta movement and the colonial period on the country's cultural and ar-

tistic roots. *Tue–Sun 9am–5pm | Admission US$8/£6.15 | Sam Sharpe Square | montegobayculturalcentre.org*

MONTEGO BAY
MARINE PARK ★

Jamaica's first marine national park was founded around Montego Bay. Fishing in this area is strictly prohibited. In return, a great underwater area invites you to dive and snorkel. So if you want to get acquainted with the indigenous submarine fauna and flora in Montego Bay during your stay, then this is your ideal destination. Water sport enterprises licensed by the supervising authority, such as *CJay's Watersports (daily 9am–5pm | Pier 1 Marina | Tel. 876 8 81 75 85 | www.cjwatersportsjm.com)*, offers sailing, snorkelling and diving excursions. *Park management Mon–Fri 9am–5pm, Sat 9am–4pm | Tel. 876 9 52 56 19 | www.mbmot.org*

SAM SHARPE SQUARE

Wooden houses in the Georgian style surround the cobbled central square, which bears the name of the Jamaican fighter for the freedom of the slaves. The statue by sculptor Kay Sullivan, cast in bronze, shows Sharpe surrounded by African slaves. The Christmas revolt he co-initiated in 1831 was brutally suppressed; more than 1000 participants were executed, and the leader was hanged on the square. Right next to the monument, The Cage recalls the time when slaves worked like animals on the whites'

JAMAICAN LEGEND

The lank youth was born musical, as his mother was not only a grocer, but also performed as a singer. Born in Nine Mile, St Ann, in 6.2.1945, the reggae musician-to-be was baptised Robert Nesta Marley. The fact that the father was a British colonial captain turned into a scandal and cost him his job. Little Marley grew up in Trenchtown, a Kingston ghetto that was a hotbed of music. At the age of 16 he recorded his first song, but the band he and Peter Tosh and Bunny Wailer founded two years later ('The Wailers') had little success for two years. The international breakthrough only came when Marley and the band released the album 'Natty Dread' in 1974. Songs like 'Stir it up', 'I shot the sheriff' and 'Get up, stand up' made him immortal and reggae world famous. The Rastafarian hit out at the social inequities of his home country and stood up for the rights of blacks and the oppressed. Thanks to the yellow press, we have world-changing knowledge of his virility. He has recognised eleven children, many of whom have followed in his musical footsteps. About 36 mothers still claim that the reggae man impregnated them. He fell sick with cancer and went to Germany for treatment, but it was too late. Having become a legend during his lifetime, he died during an in-between landing in Miami on his way back home on 11 May 1981. He was buried in Nine Mile on his mother's property.

Rebuilt after an earthquake: the St James Parish Church

plantations. The small building of clinkers and stone was erected in 1806. The dungeon was used to lock up vagrants, drunks, escaped slaves and slaves picked up after the curfew. In those days, Montego Bay had to be free of slaves after 3pm on Sundays.

ST JAMES PARISH CHURCH

No stone was left standing on another. After the severe earthquake of 1957, the limestone walls of the parish church was just a pile of rubble. Sixty years after its collapse, the church – of which the cornerstone had been laid by wealthy plantation owners in 1775 – was restored to its former glory, a particularly successful example of the late Georgian style. The church pews, carved in mahogany, and the stained-glass windows with the crucifixion scene were also restored. *Church Street/Payne Street*

WHERE TO GO

GREENWOOD GREAT HOUSE

Living in a museum: Ann and Bob Betton made this dream come true. By day, the mansion of the Barrett family, which was completed in 1800 and has a veranda from which **INSIDER TIP** one has a 180-degree panoramic view, radiates the untouchability of a museum; by night, the barrier ropes are removed and the rooms are returned to their regular state of daily use. The family home of the very wealthy Barretts was not burned down during the slave rebellion of 1831; the original fittings and fixtures remained intact. *Daily 9am–8pm, last tour 5pm | Admission US$20/£15.40 including guide | 435 Belgrade Av. | www.greenwoodgreathouse.com | 23 km/14.3 mi east of Montego Bay*

You can climb up here: Dunn's River Falls

ROSE HALL GREAT HOUSE ★

There's some serious haunting going on in the imposing mansion of the 18th century. Sex and drugs were popular in those days when Annee Palmer was carrying on here, much to the regret of her three husbands and several slaves. She ensured their premature demise with poison. Since her death, the disreputable lady is said to haunt the house as the 'white witch'. So watch your step in this tourist attraction, which was renovated at great expense in the 1960s. *Daily 9am–6pm | Admission US$20/£15.40 | on the main road to Falmouth, 14 km/8.6 mi east of Montego Bay | rosehall.com*

SHOPPING

Frequently overlooked, the *Fustic Market* is located on the route of the former station, south of Barnett Street. Besides medicinal herbs, vegetables and foodstuffs, there are woven baskets and coasters on offer. Right in the centre lies the *Montego Bay Craft Market*, at the start of the Hip Strip of the *Old Fort Craft Market*, on which the indigenous artists and crafters exhibit their wares. In the *Gallery of West Indian Art (11 Fairfield Road)* paintings of Jamaican artists, carvings, prints and handicrafts are sold.

FOOD & DRINK

INSIDER TIP CHABAD KOSHER HOT SPOT

The Israeli and Israeli-Jamaican dishes are kosher, but also vegan. Hummus and falafel, especially jerk-falafel, are regional specialities that are in great demand. *Mon–Thu 10am–8.30pm, Fr 10am–2.30pm, Sun 1am–8.30pm | 1–3 Gloucester Av. | Tel. 876 4 52 32 23 | www.jewishjamaica.com | Budget–Moderate*

HOUSEBOAT GRILL

The houseboat restaurant is located in a unique setting – it is moored in a lagoon. Part INSIDER TIP of the bottom is glazed, allowing you to see rays and barracuda. On the upper deck you can sip your cocktail and savour the view of the sea. *Southern Cross Blvd. | Montego Freeport | Tel. 9 79 88 45 | Moderate*

THE NATIVE

Specialities such as the dessert *duckunoo* are served on a stone terrace, in the shade of the trees. *29 Gloucester Ave. | Tel. 9 79 27 41 69 | Moderate*

OCHO RIOS

(📖 5/E4) **Eight rivers – that is what the Spanish name means.**
This is just a tad exaggerated, however; actually, only three small rivers mouth in the bay at this small town (pop. about 10,000) in the north of Jamaica. The town is situated in a picturesque setting, facing green forested hills that offer a first glimpse of Jamaica's natural diversity.

SIGHTSEEING

KONOKO FALLS AND PARK
More than a botanical garden: Here you experience not only Jamaica's luxuriant vegetation, but also indigenous birds. *Daily 8am–4.30pm| Admission US$20/£15.40, children (3–12 years) US$10/£7.70 | New Buckfield | www.konokofalls.com*

REGGAE HILL
Fans of Jamaican rhythms park themselves on a chair amidst colourful plants in a park-like landscape above Ocho Rios, order a cool drink, listen to the cool reggae sounds and marvel at the virtuosity of the Jamaican dancers. *White River Pines | www.reggaehill.com*

WHERE TO GO

BRIMMER HALL PLANTATION TOURS
(📖 5/E4)
This was the lordly lifestyle on Jamaica in the 18th century – if you owned a plantation and lived off the sweat of your slaves. The plantation is still operating, but without slaves (of course!). Inside, the exquisite antiquities from the era of its construction are displayed, while small businesses that sell indigenous products have moved into the former stables. *Saint Mary Parish | Tel. 87 69 94 23 09*

DUNN'S RIVER FALLS *(📖 5/E4)*
Ever clambered up a waterfall? No? Then it's high time to catch up, and you can do it on the more than 180 m/518 ft high Dunn's River Falls, which plunge directly into the sea. *Daily 8.30am–4pm, if there are cruise ships in the Ocho Rios port 7am–4pm | Admission US$23/£17.7, children US$15/£11.54 | Approx. 7 km/4.4 km east of Ocho Rios | www.dunnsriverfallsja.com*

NINE MILES *(📖 5/E4)*
A must for Bob Marley fans who stop over at Ocho Rios: the legendary musician was born here, meditated here and was laid to rest here as well. Visitors can take a guided tour and enter the mausoleum where he is interred, his guitar is also there.

BERTHS

▶ **MONTEGO BAY**
In Montego Bay the cruise ships moor in the free port about 5 km/3 mi from the city centre, which can be reached in a taxi or shuttle bus.

▶ **OCHO RIOS**
The port of Ocho Rios has two berths for cruise ships. From Reynold's Pier, also called James Bond Pier, the city centre can be reached on foot in about 15 minutes. Taxis are also available The Turtle Bay Pier is in the immediate vicinity of the city centre.

DOMINICAN REPUBLIC

If you visit the Dominican Republic, you meet the world's history.

Did you know that this is where the conquest of America started, that it was Columbus who called the island that is now shared by the Dominican Republic and Haiti Hispaniola? At that time, several million people, the Taíno, already inhabited the island. The discoverer called them Indians, because he believed he was in India. Their magical signs still decorate many of the island's caverns. However, Columbus did not spend much time on the island. Therefore little has remained from that time: the foundation walls of his first city, La Isabela, and the ruins of La Vega Vieja. As far as the Spaniards were concerned, he had done his duty by finding the western route to 'India'. The conquest and the colonisation they preferred to do themselves.

The present Dominicans are a self-aware, even proud people, and not for no reason: besides a history rich in tradition, the country also has stunning landscapes and one-of-a-kind beaches, such as the many romantic sandy bays of the Samaná peninsula or the Playa Dorada of Puerto Plata.

SANTO DOMINGO

Today the capital city of the Dominican Republic, whose approximately 3 million residents make it the largest city in the Caribbean, is a global metropolis with a brightly lit mile of luxury hotels along the Malecón, with upmarket shopping centres (called 'plazas' here) in the new town, with city highways and even an underground.

In the 16th century, Santo Domingo de Guzmán, which is the modern name of the city in full, was the most important town in the Spanish colonies. Bartolomé Columbus, the brother of the great discoverer, founded the town of Nueva Isabel, which was destroyed by a storm soon after, on the western side of the Río Ozama. The new town built on the western bank was the start of the present Santo Domingo. Before they moved to Mexico City, this was where the viceroys resided who governed the Spanish countries in the New World in the name of the Catholic Majesties. Here ships loaded with silver gathered for their long voyage back home, from here the conquistadores sallied forth in search of new countries, treasure and marvels. But the city has also experienced catastrophes and bad luck. For example, at the end of the 16th century the English circumnavigater of the world, Francis Drake, sacked the city by order of his Protestant queen Elizabeth I and left behind little more than a field of rubble. In 1992 the Faro Colón, a gigantic gravestone in the form of a cross, was erected as the symbol of the city in honour of Columbus.

SIGHTSEEING

ACUARIO NACIONAL

The fine aquarium lies directly on the Caribbean coast. Covering 2450 m^2/29,302 yards, it vividly displays the indigenous marine flora and fauna. Of course, there is also a shark section with an acrylic tunnel, and there is an impressive skeleton of a humpback whale and a theme park for children.

Tue–Sun 9.30am–5.30pm | Admission 180 pesos/£2.73 | Av. España 75 | www. acuarionacional.gob.do

CALLE EL CONDE (📍 8/B3)

This is the Old Town promenade par excellence: the pedestrian street Calle

CALLE LAS DAMAS (📍 8/B3)
AND PLAZA DE ESPAÑA (📍 8/B2)

The road of the noble Spanish ladies! Family crests carved in stone, heavy doors and low terracotta roofs – on the Calle Las Damas the oldest houses of Santo Domingo stand side by side. In the days

It was not Christopher, but his son Diego Colón who resided in the Alcázar de Colón

El Conde. If you are hungry, you will find any number of fast food outlets here between souvenir and other little shops. Benches invite you to take a break, and at the very end, at the *escalinitas* (little steps), there are free jazz concerts, *'Noches de Jazz en la Zona'* every Thursday from 8 o' clock. The old gate, the *Puerta del Conde*, is at the opposite end on a roundabout and protects a national shrine: the *Parque de la Independencia* with the cenotaphs of Duarte, Sánchez and Mella, the fathers of the republic.

of yore, Vice-Queen María de Toledo and her ladies-in-waiting attracted the greatest attention when they strolled to the cathedral or back to the Alcázar. Do accompany them on their way back: at the gate to the former Fort *Fortaleza Ozama* with the ⚜ *Torre del Homenaje (Tue–Sun 9am–5pm | Admission 70 pesos/£1)*, from which you get a great view, you are greeted by the royal chronicler Gonzalo Fernández Oviedo, and next to him, in the Casa Bastidas – now the Museo Infantil Trampolín (see box 'Travel with kids') – the discoverer of Colombia, Rodrigo de

Bastidas. Diagonally across the street, the later conqueror of Mexico, Hernán Cortés, is perhaps leaving his house (now the French embassy) and hurries to the houses of the founder of the city, Nicolás de Ovando, and the councillor Diego de Dávila, which now together form the Hotel Hodelpa Ovando. The sundial next to the Dávilas' private chapel ensured the punctuality of the audiences in the first town hall and the court building, the *Real Audiencia (Tue–Sat 9am–5pm, Sun 9am–4pm | Admission 100 pesos/£1.5)*. It now houses the museum of the city's early history. And there you are at your destination: the Plaza de España with the port tower in the city wall and in between the *Alcázar de Colón (Tue–Sat 9am–5pm, Sun 9–4pm | Admission 100 pesos/£1)*, the residence of the first Spanish viceroy of America. Actually, this title belonged to Columbus, but it was only granted to his son and heir Diego Colón. Inside, look out for the Spaniards' many souvenirs from Europe! In the evenings the palace is splendidly illuminated as on a stage, and in the boulevard cafés opposite the public pushes and shoves (especially on Fridays and Saturdays) when from 8–9pm part of the square becomes a stage for fiery folk and flamenco dancers in historic costumes under the slogan *Santo Domingo de Fiesta*.

CATEDRAL SANTA MARÍA LA MENOR
(*8/B3*)

Everything in the Old Town centres around it: America's oldest cathedral in the Parque Colón. It is believed that way back in 1510 Diego de Colón laid its cornerstone. In 1546 the Pope elevated it to the 'Catedral Primada de América'. The main entrance is decorated with ornate stone carvings. In 1887, Padre Billini discovered in this church the (purported) remains of Columbus, for which the Faro a Colón was erected to commemorate the 500th anniversary of the discovery of

The botanical garden was laid out with the greatest care

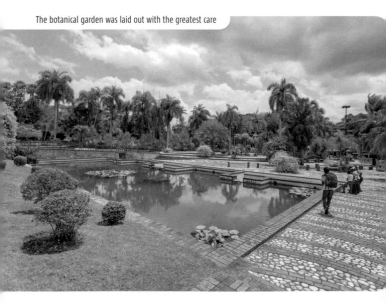

America. *Mon–Sat 9am–4.30pm | Audioguide 60 pesos/£0.90*

FUNDACIÓN GARCÍA-AREVALO
Only for those interested in ancient American archaeology: among the exquisitely detailed exhibits there are also rare INSIDER TIP ceramics of an erotic nature. *Mon–Fri 9am–5pm | Free admission | Av. San Martín 279 | in the Pepsi-Cola building*

JARDÍN BOTÁNICO
The whole garden is laid out with the same loving care as the clock of flowers at the entrance, with a natural history museum, water plant pavilion, herb, orchid and Japanese gardens as well as a river with a waterfall that runs into the Río Isabela. You can comfortably explore it with a little railway. *Daily 9am–5pm | Admission $5/£0.76 | Av. República de Colombia | www.jbn.gob.do*

PARQUE DE LOS TRES OJOS
The main attraction of the three-part, 16 m/52 ft deep cave on the eastern edge of the city is the trip on a raft across a subterranean lake. Rare plants flourish in the dark, humid climate, and it is home to many bats. *Daily 8am–5pm | Admission 100 pesos/£1.52 | Av. Las Américas/Parque Mirador del Este*

PLAZA DE LA CULTURA
Experiencing art can be as simple as this – evidently, a practical approach has been followed here. Next to the Teatro Nacional are the three museums that are probably the country's most important, all together on this large, beautiful square: the *Museo de Arte Moderno (Mon–Fri 10am–6pm | Admission 50 pesos/£0.76)*, which with works such as Eligio Pichardo's 'El sacrificio del chivo' or 'La vida de los campesinos' by José Vela Zanetti reflect the state of Domini-

can art. The *Museo del Hombre Dominicano (Tue–Sun 9am–5pm | Admission 100 pesos/£1.52)* details the country's multi-ethnic society. And in the brilliantly modernised *Museo Nacional de Historia Natural (Tue–Sun 9am–5pm| Admission 50 pesos/£0.76 | mnhn.gov.do)* one is received by the INSIDER TIP burbling and whistling noises of singing whales and can admire the giant skeletons, among others. *Av. Máximo Gómez/ Av. Pedro Henríquez Ureña*

FOOD & DRINK

EL CONUCO
An institution, because the eating culture of the country simply cannot be served up in a more captivating way: the traditional Dominican fare is often accompanied by a temperamental dance show – merengue or bachata, of course.

TRAVEL WITH KIDS

A simulated earthquake in the Planet Earth hall, generating energy yourself with a bicycle or studying the stars in the Hall of the Universe and marvelling at the muscles or blood vessels on life-size plastic people: not only children are fascinated by this fantastically presented magic world of the Museo Infantil Trampolín! There's no lack of fun either, for example with the distorting mirrors. *Tue–Fri 9am–5pm, Sat/Sun 10am–5pm | Admission 100 pesos/£1.5, children 60 pesos/£0.9 | C/ Las Damas | Casa Bastidas | trampolin.org.do*

C/ Casimiro de Moya 152 | Tel. 809 6 86 01 29 | www. elconuco.com.do | Daily | Budget–Moderate

EL MESÓN DE LA CAVA

An absolute must, already because of the ambience alone: the restaurant lies 50 ft underground in a natural, romantically illuminated cave. Against this backdrop of rock walls and chandeliers, Dominican specialities with fish and seafood are served, but international dishes as well. Popular choice: the *brunch dominical (675 pesos/£10.22)* Sundays from noon. *Av. Mirador Sur 1 | Tel. 809 5 33 28 18 | www. elmesondelacava. com | Expensive*

INSIDER TIP TIME (*8/B3*)

This is how good food without meat can be! Add the view of the relaxed doings on the Plaza Billini – a feel-good address for vegetarians! *C/ Padre Billini/C/ Arzobispo Meriño | Tel. 809 6 84 31 71 | Closed in the afternoons | Moderate*

SHOPPING

BERNSTEIN & LARIMAR (*8/B2–3*)

The shops of Jorge Caridad offer a wide selection of amber and larimar jewellery and stones, besides lovingly designed showrooms declared 'museums' *(free admission)*: the *Museo Mundo de Ámbar (C/ Arzobispo Meriño 452 | www. amberworldmuseum.com)* for amber and the *Museo de Larimar (C/ Isabel La Católica 54 | Tel.8096865700)*. The small museum *(free admission)* is waiting for you on the top floor; among other things, there is an enormous larimar on display.

ART

Art from an expert? That can run into money – but the well-established *Galería de Arte Nader (C/Rafael Augusto Sánchez/C/ Federico Geraldino)* is always worth a look. Young Dominican craftsmen and selected arts and crafts are presented by the **INSIDER TIP** *Galería Bolós (General Cabral #17 | galeriabolos.blogspot. com)*. More information on galleries is found on Facebook under Aga Dominicana.

ARTS & CRAFTS, CIGARS & RUM

The largest selection of Dominican rums and cigars – besides a whole floor of tasteful arts and crafts – is offered by the *Kenoff International Plaza* in the *Calle Arzobispo Meriño 206*. There is an *antiques market (Plaza María de Toledo)* every weekend from 8pm next to the *Panteón Nacional*. All sorts of curiosities, junk and bargains can be found on the *Mercado Modelo (Av. Mella 505)* on the outskirts of the Old Town.

WHERE TO GO

LAS SALINAS (*7/B3*)

If the duration of your stay permits, you should visit Las Salines, about 100 km west of Santo Domingo, where a surprisingly different landscape awaits you: the **INSIDER TIP** *dunes of the nature park*

ATLANTIS STONE

Larimar stone is found only in the Dominican Republic. For love of his daughter Lari, and because the stone is bright blue like the sea ('mar' in Spanish),a mine owner changed its name from travelina to Larimar. Esoterics, who credit the stone with a relaxing effect and stimulation of creativity, call it Atlantis stone. Mineralogists describe it as blue pectolith.

Las Dunas de las Calderas (Admission 100 pesos/£1.52). From the ☀ observation tower you get a great view of the bay and the dunes. On the promontory at Las Salinas, you can see how salt is recovered from salt pans. There are several fish restaurants where you can drop in.

LA ROMANA

(ⅢⅡ 7/D3) Whistling sugar trains and a busy labourers' city (pop. 202,000), on one side, the Casa de Campo with its golf courses, luxury villas and the arts town of Altos de Chavón on the other side, and in between the Río Dulce, which flows into the sea here. La Romana offers exciting contrasts.

The sugar factory, which is more than a century old *(centralromana.com.do)* is one of the country's largest employers. The founder, the Puerto Rico Sugar Company, sold the business to the US group Gulf & Western in 1967. This group then opened up the managers' residential region to tourism – the luxury resort Casa de Campo was developed, followed by the international airport and a cruise ship terminal. *explorelaromana. com*

Only old in front: St Stanislaus Church in Altos de Chavón

SIGHTSEEING

ALTOS DE CHAVÓN ★ ☀ (ⅢⅡ 7/D3)

Although it was only developed in the 1970s, the artists' town very successfully creates the impression of a settlement of the Spanish colonial period. The various small buildings accommodate studios and workshops as well as businesses selling the works of artists and craftsmen, and there are restaurants as well. There is also a good cigar shop *(Casa Montecristo Cigar Lounge)*. You should also have a look at the huge amphitheatre. The *Museo Arqueológico Regional (daily 8am–9pm | Free admission)* provides interesting information and a collection about life in the Taíno era that is worth seeing. *A few kilometres east of the hotel complex lies the Casa de Campo | www.altosdechavon. com.*

WHERE TO GO

CUEVA DE LAS MARAVILLAS ★ (ⅢⅡ 7/D3)

About 25 km/15 mi west of La Romana lies the 'Cave of marvels'. Embedded in a botanical garden, complete with visitors' centre, elevator, ramps for the handicapped and a museum path of 240 m/263 yds with automatic lighting, it outshines all other caves of the country. The 500 magical rock drawings, more than 1000 years old, of the original Taíno make this cave an archaeological treasure. *Tue–Sun*

9am–5pm | Admission 300 pesos/£4.58 | Autovía del Este, between La Romana and San Pedro de Macorís

HIGÜEY (*7/D3*)

The provincial capital (pop. 140,000), approx. 40 km/25 mi north-east of La Romana, was built in 1494, only two years after Columbus had discovered the New World, which makes it one of the oldest settlements of the New World. The pilgrimage church, *Nuestra Señora de la Altagracia*, in which the patron saint of the Dominican Republic is venerated, is well known.

ISLA CATALINA (*7/D3*

The island of barely 10 km²/3.9 mi² encompasses all the variants of an insular ecosystem, which is why the island and all its western reefs and the submarine cliff 'The Wall' in the southern side were declared a large national park. The greatest drawcard, however, is three heavenly beaches. Divers can look forward to a wreck only 3 m/13 ft down that was dis-

covered in 2007. It is thought to be the Quedagh Merchant of the pirate Captain William Kidd (1645–1701).

SANTA BÁRBARA DE SAMANÁ

(*7/C–D2*) **The capital of the eponymous peninsula in the north-east of the Dominican Republic was founded in 1756 by families that had emigrated from the Canary Islands.** After a devastating fire in 1946, Samaná was completely rebuilt. With its observation towers on the promenade at the ferry port and the 60 m/197 ft bridge that links the offshore Cayos La Vigia and Linares, Samaná, as the locals call the provincial capital (pop. 54,000), is a particularly pretty picture. That it was populated in the 19th century by slaves liberated in the USA is borne out by the Protestant churches in the town, which lies partly on steep slopes. And on the market one can still hear the English dialect of the older residents. By day the

A unique experience: encounter with a humpback whale

COME SHAKE A LEG

Jamaica has its reggae, Trinidad its calypso and the Dominican Republic the merengue – which one cannot fail to hear wherever there are people and radios round. Merengue hass an upbeat, sometimes polka-like two-four time. At the end of the 19th century, merengue was still a dance of the Dominican upper crust. Today the whole world is dancing it, not least due to the internationally successful Dominican group 4:40 (cuatro cuarenta). It also turned the bachata into a success story. Well-known interpreters of this genre, which mostly expresses the pains of love in two-four time, are Frank Reyes and Luis Vargas, among others. Among the older generation, the strongly rhythmic bolero is especially popular.

peaceful life of the town unfolds on the coastal promenade, the malecón, of the port. In the harbour the fishing boats bob up and down, and this is also from where the boats to the national park Los Haïtises and the ferries to Sabana de la Mar depart. The nearby island Cayo Levantado, with its white, sandy beach, is a popular picnic spot.

SIGHTSEEING

HUMPBACK WHALES ★
If you have the good fortune to arrive in the Dominican Republic between January and March, you may witness a fascinating natural phenomenon. By mid-January these marine mammals, up to 15 m long and weighing 30 - 40 t, arrive in Samaná Bay from the North Atlantic to mate, bear their young and nurse them until they are strong enough for the return journey starting in March. In order to protect the animals, the nature protection organisation CEBSE developed guidelines for the boatmen. Information in the *Museo de la Ballena (Mon–Sat 8am–noon and 2pm–4pm | Admission 100 pesos/£2.51| Av. La Marina/Tiro al Blanco)*. Kim Bedall of *Whale Samaná (tel. 809 5 38 24 94 |*

www.whalesamana.com) is an experienced operator.

WHERE TO GO

CAYO LEVANTADO
Samaná's dream beach has to be conquered by boat: it lies in the bay on the small offshore island. Cayo Levantado used to be a pirate hide-out, then it became the location for a Bacardi advertising shoot, and lastly it was occupied by a hotel group. But the western part of the island remains public domain, and it's definitely worth an excursion (individually from the ferry harbour, price negotiable)!

LAS TERRENAS ★
About 20 km/12.5 mi to the west, on the northern coat of the Samaná peninsula, lies the quiet town of Las Terrenas (pop. approx. 13,000). After a breathtaking drive over the range of hills in the interior of the peninsula, you drive down to the coast and reach the picturesque, sickle-shaped Playa Bonita amidst palm fields and banana plantations. In the INSIDER TIP *Haitian Caraibes Art Gallery (Calle Principal 159)* you can buy extraordinary sculptures, Haitian paintings, voo-

Cableway on the Pico Isabel de Torres

doo pictures and cigars (with their own brand).

LOS HAÏTISES ★ ◎
The national park lies approx. 20 km/12.5 mi south of the bay of Samaná and can only be reached by boat, either from Samaná or via Sabana de la Mar. The park is a karst and mangrove area, in the channels, estuaries and meanders of which numerous bird species can be observed. Not only birders, but plant lovers as well will make their discoveries here.

SABANA DE LA MAR
The former fishing village now has a population of about 15,000 and is a small, but still pleasantly peaceful tourist centre. It lies opposite Samaná, about 20 km/12.4 mi away on the southern side of the bay. Nearby there are lovely beaches, such as the Bahía de la Jina.

PUERTO PLATA

(𝄞 7/C2) **Puerto Plata (pop. 146,000) is the largest city on the northern coast of the Dominican Republic and has, despite its size, retained a certain nostalgic charm**. If not earlier, this is borne out by an unhurried stroll across the historic Calle Beller with its beautifully decorated little Caribbean houses, a visit to the Parque Central or a drive on the wave-lashed malecón to the Parque Turístico y Paisajístico de La Puntilla with the ancient fortification against pirates, Fort San Felipe. And a literally uplifting experience is waiting for you on the cableway up the local mountain Pico Isabel de Torres. Don't miss it! The city, founded in 1495, flourished when the Spanish toll regulations were abolished and president

GUM JURASSIC

Small cause, major effect: when in the amber museum of Puerto Plata Michael Crichton saw the many inclusions of insects, leaves and even small vertebrates in amber millions of years old, this is said to have sparked the idea of his best-seller Jurassic Park: to revive prehistoric animals by means of DNA analysis. Dominican amber is particularly clear and exceptionally rich in inclusions. It was formed about 50 million years ago and is nothing more than a fossilised drop of tree gum from the deciduous trees of the northern cordilleras that here and there preserved a mysterious world of prehistoric insects and dragonflies, even frogs and geckos.

Gregorio Luperón (1838–1898) governed the country from Puerto Plata. The old station of the Santiago–Puerto Plata line at the port and the Glorieta pavilion in the Parque Central, among others, date from this time. Today it is the capital city of the large province of Puerto Plata. The whole coast around Puerto Plata is generally called the amber coast *(costámbar)*, but the name is misleading: the sources of amber lie in the mountains. *www.discoverpuertoplata.com, popreport.com*

SIGHTSEEING

FORTALLZA SAN FELIPE ★

The small fort, built in 1502 and defiantly armed with bulwarks in 1541, was intended to protect the port against pirates, but later served mainly as a prison, among others of the father of the country, Pablo Duarte, after Santana's coup. Inside a military museum was created with weapons from the time of the wars of liberation. Next to the fort a memorial stone was erected for the victims of the Birgenair aircraft that crashed at Puerto Plata in 1996. *Tue–Sun 9.30am–4.45pm | Admission 100 pesos/£1.51 | La Puntilla*

MUSEO DEL ÁMBAR

In the amber museum you can admire termites, ants, leaves, flowers or roots, even birds' feathers and limbs of an iguana locked up in fossil tree gum for millions of years. The museum is housed in the magnificent former Villa Bentz that was built in 1918 for Augusto Bentz, son of the Bremen trader Emil Bentz, who had immigrated in 1865. *Mon–Sat 9am–6pm | Admission 50 pesos/£0.75 | C/ Duarte 61| www. ambermuseum.com*

PICO ISABEL DE TORRES ★ ☆

The local mountain of Puerto Plata, 793 m/2602 ft high, is accessible by cableway,

the *teleférico (daily 8.30am–5pm/350 pesos/£5.31 | Av. Circunvalación)*. Like in Rio de Janeiro, a statue of Christ was erected on top. In the nature park at the top, you can admire rare plants on long walks.

BERTHS

▶ SANTO DOMINGO

Santo Domingo has two berths for cruise ships. From the Don Diego Quay, the old centre of Santo Domingo can be reached on foot. The other berth, the Sans Souci Pier, has a modern terminal somewhat farther on. The best option for passengers is to take a taxi to the centre.

▶ LA ROMANA

Cruise ships moor either in the La Romana port, from which it is a 15-minute walk to the city centre, or at the island Isla Catalina off the coast. From here passengers are taken ashore in tenders.

▶ PUERTO PLATA/ AMBER COAST

The cruise terminal Turistica Amber Cove is the newest cruise terminal of the Dominican Republic and has two berths for cruise ships. The terminal lies approx. 12 km/7.5 mi west of Puerto Rico. To get there, taxis and rental cars are available in the port.

▶ SANTA BÁRBARA DE SAMANÁ

Cruise ships anchor in the Samaná bay; passengers are taken ashore in tenders.

PUERTO RICO

'Welcome to America!' Puerto Rico (pop. 3.7 million) leaves no doubt about it: you are on American soil.

Beyond San Juan, the capital city, the Spanish heritage is much more in evidence, without the superficial gloss of the metropolis of San Juan. Even if in the smallest villages Detroit's street cruisers set the scene, here even the English language does not get you anywhere; without Spanish, you're lost.

skyscrapers fill the business centres, here the dollar is king. Yet in this city the friendly openness of the US Americans goes hand in hand with the effervescent temperament of the population of Spanish origin. It's easy to make contact, especially if you can speak a few sentences in Spanish.

SIGHTSEEING

OLD TOWN ★ (*(ll)* 9/B-C2–3)

San Juan's Old Town is one large open-air museum, and in this regard is is reminiscent of Old Havana or the Old

The fort of San Felipe del Morro is the symbol of San Juan

SAN JUAN

The capital, Puerto Rico (pop. approx. 400,000), is partly Florida, partly New York, partly historic Spain – all under the Caribbean sun.

The traffic here roars as in innumerable other US metropolises, where you often hardly dare cross the street. Here

Town of Santo Domingo. Here, as there, the heritage of the Spaniards lives on; the former colonial power has left an unmistakable mark on the faces of these cities. For determined visitors, the fortificationa San Felipe del Morro (*daily 9am–4pm | Admission US$5/£3.81*) on the northern tip of the peninsula, which was erected by Spaniards to protect the port, is at the top of the list. After a tour of the complex, which covers several levels and with its passages, cellars, roofs, open spaces, towers and dungeons resembles a small city, it is easy to conclude that El Morro must have been a tough nut for any attacker to crack. The second fort protected San Juan against land-based assaults. ⚜ *San Cristóbal (daily 9am–4pm | Admission US$5/£3.81)*, of the 18th century, was built more recently and never fell into the hands of an enemy. The Old Town's third fortification, *La Fortaleza (Mon–Fri 9am–5pm, except on public holidays)* is the residence of the present governor of the island, the latest in a long series of more than 170 incumbents in charge of the fortunes of the island. The city's oldest building, actually the oldest remaining house in Puerto Rico, is the former residence of the descendants of Ponce de León, the first governor, the INSIDER TIP *Casa Blanca (Wed–Sun 9am–4.30pm | Admission US$3/£2.31/ Calle San Sebastián 1)*, near El Morro. At the Callejón de la Capilla, a typical Old Town alley, you will find the Casa de Callejón, a colonial house from the 18th century, which accommodates the Museo de la Arquitectura Colonial and the Museo de la Familia Puertoriqueña. Besides the historical buildings and the narrow alleys, it is mainly the squares of the Old Town that leave an unmistakable impression. The Plaza de Colón, with a statue of the explorer Christopher Columbus, the Plaza de Armas, with the town hall and the Plaza de San José, with the eponymous church and the Dominican monastery, are beautiful to behold.

BOTANICAL GARDEN
A visit to the garden of almost 0.6 km^2/6562 yards is a good opportunity to get acquainted with the great diversity of the island's flora. Besides indigenous trees and shrubs, the garden also contains plants from other tropical and subtropical regions of the world. The collection of indigenous orchids, which is supplemented with many lovely new-bred varieties, is especially worth noting. *Daily 6am–6pm | Free admission | Barrio Venezuela | Route 1, at the Route 847 crossing*

FUERTE SAN GERÓNIMO
This small fortification was erected in 1788 on the site of an earlier defensive structure and is located near the Caribe Hilton. It's worthwhile clambering up the ⚜ walls to enjoy the view of Condado. Unfortunately, the entrance is often closed. *In the east | Puerta de Tierra*

MUSEO PABLO CASALS (𝄞 9/B2)
The house with the resonating name in which the famous Spanish cellist Pablo Casals died has been converted into a small memorial in which sheet music, musical instruments and other memorabilia are exhibited. *Tue–Sat 9.30am– 4pm | Admission US$1/£0.77 | Calle San Sebastián 101*

BERTH

▶ **SAN JUAN**
The port of San Juan has four cruise ship berths near the Old Town, which you can reach on foot from here. About 1.5 km/1 mi away is the Pan American Pier on the Isla Grande. San Juan's Old Town can be reached by taxi or bus from here.

TRAVEL TIPS

CAYMAN ISLANDS

 MONEY & CREDIT CARDS
On the Cayman Islands you pay in dollars; common credit cards and the Girocard are also accepted. Banks are usually open on Mon–Thu from 9am–4pm and Fri from 9am–4.30pm.

HEALTH
Medical care on Grand Cayman is good; foreign health insurance and an emergency kit are recommended.

TELEPHONE, MOBILE PHONE & WIFI
When making calls on the Cayman Islands, the call number directly follows the county code. Area code: 001345. Locally bought SIM cards are cheaper than using your own card. On Grand Cayman there are numerous free WiFi hotspots (info at *www.explorecayman.com*, section Discover Cayman, Travel Information).

CUBA

MONEY & CURRENCY
At present Cuba's economy is still operating with two parallel currency systems: the Cuban peso (CUP or MN) and the Peso Convertible (CUC), the foreign exchange currency, which has no value abroad. Euros can be converted into CUC at the going rate without any problems; but when exchanging US dollars for CUC a fee of 10% is charged! In most of the tourist zones the euro is also accepted in cash. It's best to travel with euros in cash; European VISA or Master cards are accepted (but the card must not be from a US bank, and EC/Maestro cards are not accepted either!). With a credit card and passport, you can get cash in the CUC at a fee of 3% in a bank. With PIN and a (European) VISA credit card, you can also draw CUC at many ATMs – provided that there are no technical problems.

HEALTH
Take a sufficient amount of the medication you need. If you need to be treated by a doctor, you pay cash in CUC. To enter the country, proof of foreign health insurance - in Spanish! – is compulsory.

INTERNET & WIFI
By now almost every town has a WiFi hotspot, usually in a public park. The state-owned telephone company Etecsa sells internet access cards for CUC2–7/£1.53–5.38 (1–5 hrs). If you do not want to access the internet via a smartphone, but a PC, you can find terminals in the Etecsa; but these are really slow.

DOMINICAN REPUBLIC

MONEY & CREDIT CARDS
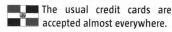 The usual credit cards are accepted almost everywhere.

HEALTH
International health insurance including repatriation is recommended in all cases. Officially, no inoculations are required for visiting the Dominican Republic.

Greater Antilles

INTERNET & WIFI

Many restaurants and cafés offer free *WiFi (WiFispc.com)*. Internet cafés usually charge 30 pesos/£0.45 per hour. There are 15 companies (Claro and Orange are the largest) that provide internet coverage for almost the whole country.

JAMAICA

MONEY & CURRENCY

The official national currency is the Jamaican dollar (J$ or JMD), which cannot be imported or exported without limitations. In areas frequented by tourists, prices are mostly stated in US dollars. When purchasing with a credit card, prices are always converted into US dollars. For smaller expenses and visits to local restaurants, its' better to have Jamaican dollars ready. Banks have branches all over the islands. Business hours: 8.30am–2.30pm, Fri 8.30am–4pm.

HEALTH

For the rainy season, be sure to have adequate insect repellents. Foreign health insurance including repatriation insurance with unlimited take-over of cost commitments is recommended. Generally, in Jamaica consultations and hospitalisation must be paid in cash. If you are properly insured, your expenses will be refunded on presentation of proof of payment.

TELEPHONE & MOBILE PHONE

For calls to Jamaica the country code is 001, then the subscriber's number without the leading 0 (as in the UK). In Jamaica, the full 10-digit number must be dialled. For calls to the UK, dial 011 44, then the UK number without its leading zero.

All European providers offer roaming; the cost per minute can be up to US$3.50/£2.60). For multiple calls, it is cheaper to buy a new SIM card with the country number (around US$3.50/£2.60).

PUERTO RICO

MONEY & CREDIT CARDS

The Puerto Rican currency is the US dollar. The customary credit cards are accepted. You can use them with your PIN number to draw money at ATMs; the Girocard is also accepted. Banks are open Mon–Fri from 9am to 4.30pm.

HEALTH

Medical care is relatively good. It is advisable to take out international health insurance, and an emergency kit is useful.

TELEPHONE, MOBILE PHONE & WIFI

For telephone calls to Puerto Rico, dial the call number immediately after the country code. Puerto Rico code: 001787. For mobile calls, a local SIM card is recommended. In San Juan many cafés and restaurants offer free WiFi.

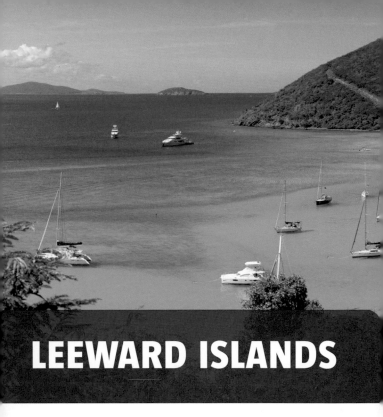

LEEWARD ISLANDS

**The Leeward Islands do not form a co-
herent geographic or political group.**
At the time when the individual islands
still formed the administrative unit of
the Leewards within the British Em-
pire, there were already a scattering of
small islands governed by France, Hol-
land or Denmark. The Leeward Islands
form the northern group of the Lesser
Antilles island chain; to the south are
the Windward Islands. Overall, the
Lesser Antilles lie on a curve about
800 km/500 mi long from the South
American coast to south-east of Puerto
Rico. Many of the islands are of volcanic origin. This is apparent not only
from the coastlines, which frequently
rise steeply from the sea, and the jag-
ged mountains in the interior, but also
from the many (often only temporar-
ily) dormant volcanoes, hot springs
and sulphurous emissions that unexpectedly rise from cracks in the rocks.
Only a few islands are flat, thereby
indicating that they were formed as
raised limestone sediments – usually
the remains of coral reefs.

BRITISH
VIRGIN
ISLANDS

**Large, small and tiny islands – in
between the sea sparkles in all conceivable hues of green and blue.**

Here the sun shines almost all the time, the sea is blue and the longing for laid-back Caribbean flair is satisfied everywhere

Columbus was already impressed by the number of islands, and he named the group after the 11,000 virgins who, in the 5th century, were said to have been the retinue of Saint Ursula. Actually, there are only about 100 islands that rise from the sea east of Puerto Rico as the most northerly group of the Lesser Antilles.

Politically, the islands are divided into two: on the eastern side, the British Virgin Islands and on the western side, the US Virgin Islands. The British Virgin Islands are quieter than their US sisters, which have been an unincorporated US territory since 1917: *going liming* (hanging out and just enjoying the tranquillity of the day) is the basic attitude. The locals have retained much shows of the British way of life, which show its best side in the subtropical climate. Today the islands are a British crown colony, i.e. the English Queen is the nominal head of state, but the islanders regulate their internal affairs largely by themselves.

TORTOLA

(𝄞 7/F3) **Tortola, the main island of the British Virgin islands (pop. 15,000), so called by the Spaniards because of its many turtle doves, lies at the northern edge of the Francis Drake Channel.**
The largest part of the island of 54 km²/20.8 mi² is covered by shrubs, as the rainforest was cleared to make room for sugar plantations. Traces of the original vegetation can only be found on Mt Sage in the western part of the island. The capital is Road Town, where the cruise ships also moor.

SIGHTSEEING

J. R. O'NEAL BOTANIC GARDENS
The botanical garden of the capital city is still young, but can already boast a lovely layout, with a small orchid house, a bamboo grove and several ponds. *Mon–Sat 9am–4.30pm | US$3/£2.3 | Road Town*

MOUNT SAGE NATIONAL PARK
Mount Sage is Tortola's highest 'mountain' (543 m/1781 ft). The national park, where the rainforest is protected, lies on its slopes. Owing to the intensive plantation industry, almost only scrub-like shrubs grow on Tortola and the other islands. The rainforest is not impressive either, but accessible on good roads. *Admission US$3/£2.3 | Ridge Road | Access from Joe's Hill Road*

ROAD TOWN
The rather ordinary little town lies on

The Baths: a somewhat sober name for a spectacular spot

a bay on the southern coast, framed by hills. Road Town is the capital city and seat of the governor and administration of the British Virgin Islands. From its busy port, ferries leave for the other islands and to St John's and St Thomas.

VIRGIN GORDA

(𝄜 7/F3) **The island (pop. 3000) lies east of Tortola, and with approx. 20 km² /7.72. mi it is the third largest of the British Virgin Islands. The landscape is rather more dry tropical; on the other hand, the Baths are a special geological attraction.**

Referring to its bulging shape, Christopher Columbus described the island as a 'fat woman' – with a little imagination, one can see his point when looking at a map. Nevertheless, the island scores with its lovely beaches and lush nature.

The remains of a copper mine remind of the British past. Here miners who arrived on the island from Cornwall extracted the ore in the south-west of Virgin Gorda. The mine are on the coast, and from here you got a great site view of the clear, blue sea. That the Spaniards were active in the Caribbean is borne out today not only by the name of the capital Spanish Town, but also the ruins of a Spanish fort.

SIGHTSEEING

THE BATHS ⭐
A number of large rocks form small pools, caves and open or covered channels – interesting spots, ideal for swimming and snorkelling. A path partly made safe by ropes leads through the rock formations, where a degree of surefootedness is required. If you master the path from

The Baths on the beach, you will get to Devil's Bay, a pretty horseshoe-shaped bay. *Daily 9am–4pm | US$3/£2.3 |southwest of Spanish Town*

SPANISH TOWN
The sleepy little capital in the south-east of the island has a fine yacht harbour with shopping arcades, pub and supermarket.

JOST VAN DYKE

(𝄜 7/F3) **The name of the smallest (only approx. 8 km² /3 mi²) of the British Virgin Islands (pop. approx. 300)**

BERTHS

▶ **TORTOLA**
On Tortola, cruise ships usually dock at the cruise ship pier in Road Town. In 2015 a modern cruise terminal was built with numerous businesses and restaurants. The centre of Road Town can be reached on foot.

▶ **VIRGIN GORDA**
On Virgin Gorda, cruise ships moor either in the port of Spanish Town or in North Sound. In Spanish Town passengers are taken to the yacht harbour by tender and in North Sound to the Bitter End Yacht Club.

▶ **JOST VAN DYKE**
Most cruise ships moor in Great Harbour; passengers are taken ashore in tenders. The town centre can be reached on foot.

In the Caribbean they like a dash of colour, even when they dine out

reminds of a Dutch pirate. The ruins of former sugar mills testify to the erstwhile importance of this economic factor.

On the car-free island north of Tortola – the main town is Great Harbour – there are a few restaurants and beach bars that are popular among sailors, e.g. the *Soggy Dollar Bar,* White Bay. Try a shot of a INSIDER TIP Painkiller, a drink that's something else!

If you are steady on your feet and would like a full view (in the truest sense of the word) of the island, you can climb to the top of *Majohnny Hill* (all of 320 m/1050 ft). It's a fairly steep climb, especially given the subtropical temperatures, which can make you sweat, but in return you will be rewarded with a ✲ spectacular 360° view. If you'd rather chill in the sun, you can choose between *Great Harbour Bay,* which is protected by a reef, and *White Bay.*

SINT MAARTEN

(🗺 10/A-B2) **Sint Maarten shares the island with its French neighbour, St-Martin. World-wide, this combination is the smallest geographic unit on which two national states live together peacefully.** The Dutch part (pop. 41,000) is a little smaller than the French part and lies in the south. Sint Maarten is the most prosperous of the Dutch Antilles. This was achieved by extensive construction for the tourist industry: large hotel complexes after the US model, restaurants, bars and casinos.

PHILIPSBURG

The capital lies on a land bridge be-

tween **Great Bay** and the **Great Salt Pond**.

The main streets, Front Street and Achterstraat, run parallel to the water. Front Street is the shopping mile, with duty-free shops, restaurants and casinos. The old Dutch courthouse is worth a look.

SIGHTSEEING

ST MAARTEN PARK
A must for children! A small zoo with Caribbean and South American animals and plants such as white lipped peccaries or cotton-top tamarins. A bat cave is home to a family of flying foxes. *Daily 9am–5pm | Admission US$10/£7.71 | Madame Estate, Arch Road*

WATHEY SQUARE
This square is the heart of Philipsburg. Its Dutch buildings, such as the town hall and the courthouse, date back to the 18th century. The hotels, restaurants and duty-free shops were built around the square as time passed.

FOOD & DRINK

L'ESCARGOT
Provençal cuisine with a dash of the Caribbean is served on the terrace surrounding the colourful gingerbread house. Besides the snails referred to in the name, there are also other delicacies! *Front St. | Tel. 721 5 42 24 83 | Expensive*

BERTH

▶ **SINT MAARTEN**
Philipsburg's cruise ship port can accommodate even the largest cruise ships. Taxis and excursion buses are available at the port.

SAINT-BARTHÉLEMY

(🕮 10/B2) **Together with Martinique and Guadeloupe, St-Barts or St-Barth (as the island is called for short) belong to the French Antilles. While Saint-Barthélemy and Guadeloupe are part of the Leeward Islands, Martinique belongs to the Windward Islands. All together, the islands belong to the French 'overseas collectivities' and are**

AT THE DROP OF A BAT

Cricket is and will remain the national sport of the English islands! The Leeward Islands, like the Windward Islands and Barbados, have teams that achieve international successes. On weekends, when the sun becomes less fierce, all the locals gather on the *local cricket ground* to cheer on their players and have their snacks. It's not important at all if one doesn't understand the rules; you come and go anyway, walk around a bit, chat or sit in the shade of a tree ...

francophone enclaves in the otherwise anglophone region.

The island of slightly more than 20 km²/7.72 mi² has a population of 8000, most of which are of Norman or Breton descent. This island also changed hands any number of times: in the 18th century it belonged to France, then Sweden and the Knights of Malta took possession of it, and in 1878 it reverted to France. Today tourism is the mainstay of the island's economy. The jetsetters of the world of politics and economy, film and music love meeting here for one huge party. The Kennedys and the Rockefellers used to own property here. Prices are correspondingly high.

GUSTAVIA

Despite the fire that raged here in 1852, the architecture of the island's capital, idyllically located on a naturally shielded bay, still displays the Swedish influence.

It was called after King Gustav III. The status of the island as a free port also dates from this period.

SIGHTSEEING

THE WALL HOUSE MUSEUM
The museum is housed in a historic building from the period of Swedish rule (1785–1878). With exhibits and documents, it is dedicated to the history of Saint-Barthélemy. *Rue de Pere Irenee de Bruyn*

WHERE TO GO

COROSSOL
The fishing village comes to life especially in the evening, when the boats come back in from the sea. On Sundays, some women still wear their traditional Norman clothes when they go to church. They sell wickerwork and other crafts. *2 km/1.2 mi north-west of Gustavia*

INTER OCEANS MUSEUM
The small museum houses a fabulous collection of shells, with wonderful specimens not only from the Caribbean, but from seas all over the world. *Tue–Sun 9am–noon and 2–5 pm| Admission eur3/£2.6 | Corossol*

ANTIGUA

(🗺 10/C2) **Antigua is the middle island of the northern Lesser Antilles and the largest of the Leeward Islands.**

The island (pop. 70,000) was discovered by Christopher Columbus in 1493; it has been owned by the British since the end of the 17th century, and there are no French influences. In the 18th century Antigua was the main naval base of the British in the Caribbean. The island has been an independent constitutional monarchy within the Commonwealth, in which the Queen is represented by a governor general. In the colonial period, Antigua was a typical sugar island with many plantations. In many places one can still see

BERTH

▶ **SAINT-BARTHÉLEMY**
Cruise ships usually anchor outside the port of Gustavia; passengers are taken ashore in tenders and can reach the centre on foot.

the ruins of the stone mills in which the sugar was pressed.

ST JOHN'S

The capital city of St John's, on the island's north-western coast, was built in the 17th century, and more than half of Antigua's population (approx. 36,000) lives there.

The historical buildings, restored in the 1980s, at the cruise ship terminal Redcliffe Quay and Heritage Quay belie the fact that the larger part of St John's is in need of rehabilitation.

SIGHTSEEING

MUSEUM OF ANTIGUA AND BARBUDA

Here you can examine the more than 10,000 years of the island's history and its origin as well as information about its inhabitants over the years. The museum shop sells, among others, pottery and antique old views of the islands. *Mon–Sat 8.30am–4.30pm | Long St | www. antiquamuseums.net*

WHERE TO GO

ENGLISH HARBOUR

In the 18th century, in a bay on the southern coast, about 20 km/12.5 mi from St John's, the English found an ideal anchorage for their Caribbeean fleet. Here the fleet was protected against storms, and from the surrounding cliffs it could also easily be protected. Today the harbour complex is one of Antigua's major tourist attractions, but the ruins of the fortifications on *Shirley Heights* are also worth a visit.

NELSON'S DOCKYARD ★

The subsequent victor of the Battle of Trafalgar served here as a young officer; later he became commander of the naval base named for him. Today the complex is an open-air museum with old storehouses and workshops, docks and residential spaces. Some have also been converted into hotels or restaurants. From the end of April to the beginning of May, Nelson's dockyard is also the headquarters of the INSIDER TIP „Antigua Sailing Week", a regatta with a genuine popular festival character. *20 km/12.5 mi southeast from St John's*

BERTH

▶ ANTIGUA

Saint John's has three berths: the Heritage Quay and the Redcliffe Quay, both within walking distance of the city centre, and the deepwater harbour about 1.5 km/0.9 mi from the centre. Taxis are available for farther travel.

GUADELOUPE

(📖 10/C–D3) **The Caribbeans were more imaginative when naming their island than Columbus: he named it after 'the holy lady of Guadeloupe' in Spain; they called it Karukera: 'Island of the pretty waters'.**

The shape of the island (pop. approx. 405,000) resembles a butterfly, with the two wings being connected only by a narrow strip of land. The smaller eastern wing is called Grande-Terre, is a relatively flat limestone plateau of coralline origin and is used for agriculture. The western half is called Basse-Terre; here there are mountains of volcanic origin up to almost 1500 m/4921 ft high. A large part of the interior of Basse-Terre is occupied by the Parc National de la Guadeloupe, which contains not only the volcano Soufrière, but also extensive rainforests. Besides the smaller offshore islands, St Martin and St-Barthélémy farther off also belong to the Département Guadeloupe.

BASSE-TERRE

The pretty little port on the south-western coast lies at the foot of the volcano La Soufrière.

Although with a population of 12,000 it is much smaller than Pointe-à-Pitre, it is nevertheless the administrative seat of the whole Département. On the narrow streets and small squares planted with palms, there are some charming buildings in the French colonial style such as the town hall, and in the south there are the ruins of *Fort Louis Delgrès* from the 17th century *(daily 9am–4.30pm | Free admission)*.

SIGHTSEEING

CATHÉDRALE NOTRE-DAME-DE-GUADELOUPE
A building was already erected on this site in 1673; the cathedral in the 'Jesuit' baroque style was built with volcanic stone in 1730. In 1825 a hurricane destroyed it, but it was rebuilt about 10 years later. Interesting detail: the bell tower is not integrated with the church building, but stands on its own.
Place Bébian

SAINT-CLAUDE
The pleasant suburb of Basse-Terre lies on the slope of the volcano *La Soufrière*. From the ☈ picnic spot in town you have a splendid view of the volcano.

WHERE TO GO

LA SOUFRIÈRE
At 1467 m/4813 ft, the still active volcano La Soufrière is not only the highest mountain of Guadeloupe, but of all the Lesser Antilles. If you have enough time during your stopover on Guadeloupe and you want to reach for the skies, you can rent a car: you can drive

DO YOU SPEAK ENGLISH?

Yes, OK, sort of. But the inhabitants of the British islands don't simply speak English. They speak 'West Indian', a melodious language that, with its own grammar and idioms, is difficult even for native English speakers. If you want to eavesdrop on locals talking to one another (and speaking very fast too), it can be quite an effort. Phrases such as *I don't know* become *me na no* in the local vernacular. *I'll see you later* shrinks to a bare *lata; the worst place* is *de wussest place*. Obviously, the islanders who get to deal with foreign guests have acquired a certain kind of 'American', with the result that problems are hardly likely to occur.

Steam still rises from the crater of the La Soufrière

up to an altitude of 1100 m/3608.9 ft, through subtropical rainforest that urges you to go and explore. To be sure, from the parking area of the *Savane à Mulets* there is still a really tough climb of 300 m/328 yards to go. Part of the way leads through cold and moist mists, which unfortunately often spoil the view of the crater.

POINTE-À-PITRE

Pointe-à-Pitre (pop. 16,000) is the economic hub of the island.

It's not a particularly attractive town, but besides some good restaurants there are plenty of shopping opportunities that are not different from European metropolises. The city centre lies around the *Place de la Victoire,* a lovely small park with shady trees on the water. This is also where the weekly market takes place, where you can feel that you are in the Caribbean and not in France.

SIGHTSEEING

MUSÉE SCHŒLCHER

The museum, housed in an attractive colonial building with wrought-iron window balconies, is dedicated to Victor Schœlcher, who in the 19th century fought for the abolition of slavery on the French Antilles. In his former residence you can see furniture, furnishings and memorabilia. *Mon–Fri 9am–5pm | Admission €3/£2.60 | Rue Peynier*

BERTH

▶ **GUADELOUPE**

On Guadeloupe cruise ships moor in the port of Pointe-à-Pitre. The centre is easily reached on foot from the large cruise terminal.

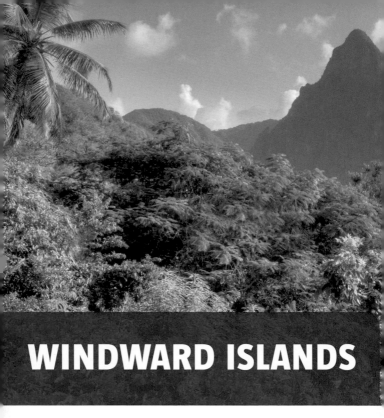

WINDWARD ISLANDS

When it comes to the geographical names of the island groups of the Lesser Antilles, one is faced with a complete mix-up. Actually, the names 'Windward' and 'Leeward' indicate the position of the islands relative to the trade winds.

Therefore the Spaniards, French and Dutch described the islands off the coast of South America as the 'downwind' *(leeward)* islands and those on the arc running from north to south down to the Greater Antilles as the 'upwind' *(windward)* islands. However, for inexplicable reasons the British decided to describe their possessions from Trinidad to St Lucia as Windward Islands and those to the north up to the Virgin Islands as Leeward Islands.

Today all islands north of Grenada and south of Dominica (including these two) are grouped together as the Windward Islands. This region of 'dormant volcanoes' has a very diverse flora and fauna. Most of the islands have nature parks with hiking and trekking paths. The smell of sulphur is present almost everywhere when you are climbing up through the rainforest.

DOMINICA

(◫ 11/B1) **Dominica may be the largest anglophone island of the Lesser Antilles, but with 73,000 inhabitants it is not as densely populated as the other islands of the Antilles. Its nature has not**

Photo: Rainforests and mountains of volcanic origin make up the Windward Islands

Beaches like sugar, subtropical climate, evidence of European influences – the Windward Islands make island dreams come true

been destroyed by industry, tourism or agriculture either and is therefore still largely intact.

Dominica was the first land Columbus saw on his second voyage to the New World. Before he sailed on northward, he gave the island the name it still bears today – Dominica, after the day of the Lord on which he saw it. Only after another 200 years did the first Frenchmen settle on Dominica. Although they lost possession of the island in the 18th century, the French influence persisted under British rule for many years thereafter. Great Britain gradually eased Dominica into independence since 1925, until in 1978 the autonomous Commonwealth of Dominica came into existence.

The interior of the country is mountainous, and its ranges still show some of the volcanic activity here and there without which the island would not have been formed. On the narrow coastline in the west of the island and in the shallow valleys of the interior, there are settlements as well as banana, coconut and citrus plantations. On the eastern slopes there are extensive rainforests, which are nourished by the moist Atlantic winds – the heavy clouds drop their loads here. The Dominican rainforest is called a layered forest, in which a multitude of other plants – ferns, palms, orchids, bromeliads and climbing plants – have established themselves below the canopies of the forest giants. These forests are home to numerous bird species, including the sisserou, a rare parrot species that has been declared the island's national bird. Unfortunately,

A tropical idyll: the Emerald Pool

this parrot, also called the imperial amazon, is threatened with extinction. The forests also host countless insect species, butterflies and beetles, which are conspicuous by their beautiful colours. There are no poisonous snakes on Dominica, but there are boa constrictors, which can reach a length of more than 4 m/13 ft. Besides smaller lizard species, the larger iguana is also found on Dominica, which – given its appearance – cannot deny its relationship with the dinosaurs. It is found especially often on the west coast.

ROSEAU

The small city (pop. 16,000) makes you feel you have been transported back into the colonial period.

No hotel blocks, few new buildings, no duty-free shops. With its colourful houses, the little city nestles against the mountains towering behind it. Roseau is the administrative and commercial centre of the islands. Farmers and businesspeople come here on official business or to sell fruit and vegetables. A walk through the Old Town is a peaceful undertaking. Saturday morning is market day at the mouth of the Roseau River in the north-western part of the city. The house in Cork Street in which the author Jean Rhys was born was a small guest house for many years, but is now closed.

SIGHTSEEING

BOTANICAL GARDEN
The 10 ha botanical garden in the southeastern part of the city was laid out more than hundred years ago on the site of a former sugar plantation. With its mighty ancient trees, it is a perfect spot to take five in the shade. *Daily 8am–4pm*

CATHEDRAL OF OUR LADY OF FAIR HAVEN

Construction of the Roman Catholic church started in the early 19th century, but it was finished only in 1916 with the western tower. The church was built with volcanic rock; the interior is furnished with Victorian pews and murals from the same period. *20 Virgin Lane*

DOMINICA MUSEUM

The museum, in close vicinity to the cruise ship quay, relates the development of the island from its origins to the first inhabitants and its more recent history. *Mon–Fri 9am–4pm, Sat 9am–noon| Admission 3 EC$/£0.86 | Dame Mary Eugenia Charles Blvd*

FOOD & DRINK

OLD STONE BAR AND GRILL

Old stone walls and many green plants give the small restaurant with its friendly service a lovely ambiance. Highly recommended: the shrimp with pineapple salsa! *15 Castle St. | Roseau | Tel. 767 4 40 75 49 | Moderate*

WHERE TO GO

EMERALD POOL

A pretty little waterfall falls into a cave surrounded by forest and invites you to have a cooling dip. *Admission US$5/£3.87 22 km / 13.5 mi north-east of Roseau*

SULPHUR SPRINGS

If during your stay you want to rent a car, the hot sulphur springs that prove Dominica's volcanic origin are an interesting destination. You can get there comfortably by car, only the last few metres it's best to do on foot. The water emerges over an area of just a few square metres. Here and there it bubbles: water

BERTH

▶ DOMINICA

In Roseau, cruise ships more near the city centre, which can be reached on foot. On the quays taxis, rental cars and minibuses are available.

and gas escape from deep down. The strong smell of sulphur already makes itself known a some distance. *Halfway between Roseau and Laudat.*

MARTINIQUE

(🕮 11/B-C1) **Martinique, which the original inhabitants called Madinia ('island of flowers'), is said to have the prettiest girls of the whole Caribbean ...**
Like many others in the region, the island (pop. approx. 400,000) has had a turbulent history. It often changed hands between Great Britain and France. The English occupied Martinique in 1762, but later swapped it back to France in exchange for Canada, Senegal, St Vincent and Tobago. With hindsight, this exchange seems rather audacious, but at the time it was quite sensible from the French point of view, as Martinique and Guadeloupe were important producers of sugar. Even today Martinique is an agriculturally intensively used island, exporting bananas and pineapples in addition to sugar and rum.

FORT-DE-FRANCE

It became the capital only in 1902, after a volcanic eruption had eradicated St-Pierre.

Today Fort-de-France is a flourishing metropolis (pop. approx. 160,000) radiating French flair. Worth seeing are the *Fort St-Louis,* which is still in military use and entrance is therefore restricted, and the fine park called *La Savane* on the *Baie des Flamands.* Here you will find the statues of Empress Joséphine (Napoleon's first wife was born on Martinique in 1763) and of the leader of the first French settlers on the island, Pierre Belain d'Esnambuc.

SIGHTSEEING

BIBLIOTHÈQUE SCHŒLCHER
Built in 1886/87 in the Historicism style, the building houses the comprehensive collection of books of Victor Schœlcher. The lovely building has been protected as a monument since the early 1990s. *Mon 1pm–5.30pm, Tue–Thu 8.30am–5.30pm, Fri 8am–5.30pm, Sat 8.30am–noon | Free admission | 1, rue de la Liberté*

MUSÉE DÉPARTEMENTAL D'ARCHÉOLOGIE ET DE PRÉHISTOIRE DE LA MARTINIQUE
The museum has exhibitions on the Indian past of Martinique and on the history of slavery. *Mon 1pm–5pm, Tue–Fri 8am–5pm, Sat 9am–noon | Admission US$4.5/£4.6 | 7, rue de la Liberté*

WHERE TO GO

CENTRE D'INTERPRÉTATION DU PATRIMOINE PAUL GAUGUIN
Almost everybody has seen them some time – those paintings of the landscape, the people and the colours on the island inspired paintings by Paul Gauguin, who spent some months on Martinique in 1887 and experienced a phase of creative activity here. The modern museum offers a multimedia insight into the artist's work. *Tue–Sat 9.30am–5pm, Sun 9.30am–3pm| Admission €8/£7.1 | Anse Turin Quartier Beauregard | 97221 Le Carbet | Approx. 32 km/19.9 mi north of Fort-de-France*

MONT PELÉE
You can reach the impressive mountain (1397 m/583 ft) in the northern part of the island by car. In the cruise harbour you can rent a taxi for the trip. Halfway up the volcano, there is a parking area with a ⚜ viewing platform, from where you get a fine view of the Atlantic. Anyone who wants to and is fit enough can climb up to the crater from here. *Approximately 44 km/27.3 mi north of Fort-de-France*

INSIDER TIP MUSÉE DU RHUM SAINT-JAMES
This museum is housed in a fine colonial building. A tour of the present distillery and rum tasting are part of the visit. *Mon–Fri 9am–5pm, Sat/Sun 9am–1pm | Free admission | Saint James Distillery | Sainte-Marie | approx. 35 km/27,7 mi north-east of Fort-de-France*

ST-PIERRE ★
Disaster struck the city on May 8 1902. The inabitants of St Pierre had simply ignored the warning rumbling of Mount Pelée in the preceding days and that all animals had fled. And suddenly, in a rain of incandescent ash the volcano transformed the capital city of Martinique into a Caribbean Pompeii in three minutes. Only one of the inhabitants is said to have survived the eruption – locked up in a cell for drunkenness.

Mount Pelée looks quite peaceful above St-Pierre

The small town that now bears the name St-Pierre stands on the site of the destroyed city. A few remains of buildings can be seen, including the life-saving prison cell. The museum provides information on the course of the catastrophe. *Daily 9am–5pm | Admission €5/£4.4 | approx. 33 km/21.7 north of Fort-de-France*

ZOO DE MARTINIQUE

Quite an unusual place for a zoo: animals from Central and South America, Australia and Africa now roam the grounds of the island's oldest house, the Habitation Latouche of 1643. The ruins of the buildings appear romantic, the lories show off their brightly coloured plumage, big cats like jaguars and pumas glide past majestically. The park restaurant offers snacks and light lunches *(11.30am–2.30pm). Daily 9am–6pm (last admission 14.30) | Admission €16.50 | Anse Latouche, Le Carbet, St-Pierre | Approx. 33 km/20.5 mi north of Fort-de-France | www. zoodemartinique.com*

BERTH

▶ **MARTINIQUE**

In Fort-de-France cruise ships usually moor at the Pointe-Simon quay, which is in the centre of the capital. There is also a berth at the Quai des Tourelles, approx. 2.5 km/1.5 mi from the centre. Excursion taxis are available a the quay.

ST LUCIA

(🗺 11/C2) **St Lucia boasts one of the symbols of the Lesser Antilles: the twin cones of the Piton mountains. Not only do they appear on numerous postcards, but also in the titles of some books about this region.**

The island (pop. approx. 173,000) is typical of the Windward Islands: it has long, sandy beaches and offshore coral reefs, tropical rainforests, a volcano and sulphurous springs as well as forest reserves to protect the indigenous *jacquot,* a parrot species, and other rare, sometimes endemic bird species. Anyone on a cruise who stops over at the island and would like to experience its breathtaking nature will find a rich

selves, is *Kwéyòl,* a variety of Patois consisting of English and French, but with its own grammar and syntax, which is incomprehensible even to West Indians from other islands.

CASTRIES

The capital city of St Lucia (pop. approx. 16,000) was destroyed almost completely in a huge fire in 1948. You are therefore unlikely to find buildings dating back to before the fire.

The *cathedral* on Columbus Square is well worth a visit, with its interior walls and ceiling decorated with colourful scenes of town life. If you happen to be in town on a Saturday morning, you should visit the weekly market at *cnr Jeremie/Peynier Street.*

The Pitons already welcome you when the ship is approaching

offering, ranging from guided or unguided hikes through the tropical forest to all water sports and observation of whales and tortoises.

The language of the *Lucies* (pronounced *Looshies*), as the inhabitants call them-

WHERE TO GO

LUSHAN COUNTRY LIFE PARK

A visit to the Lushan Country Life Park is a good alternative to lazing about on the beach. With local guides you pass through the rainforest and the beautifully laid out gardens and on to the traditional houses. In the process, you learn a lot about the history of St Lucia, its traditions and nature. At every stop, various things are explained: herbs, spices, tropical birds or seasonal fruit. Creole specialities are also supplied as finger food.

PIGEON ISLAND

This island, connected to St Lucia by a dam, has been a witness to history time and again: remains of original Indian inhabitants have been found here, the pirate Jambe de Bois (Wooden Leg) hid himself in a cave, Admiral Rodney set sail from here in 1782 to fight the French. Ruins and forts testify to the turbulent past. The two beaches invite you to take a dip, there is a restaurant and there are picnic spots. The museum in the officers' mess provides information about historical events.

PITONS ⭐

The symbols of the island are on the south-western coast, south of *Soufrière*. Here the *Gros Piton* and the *Petit Piton* rise up directly on the shore: sharp cones of volcanic origin that reach a height of more than 700 m/2300 ft. Experienced mountain hikers or mountaineers can attempt an ascent, but should definitely get a guide in Soufrière. *From Soufrière on the road to towards Choiseul*

RAINFOREST OF FOND ST JACQUES

The town of Fond St Jacques is surrounded by a still relatively intact rainforest area. Here there are still specimens of the rare *St Lucia parrot (Amazona versicolor)*.

GOLDEN ZIPLINE

Venturesome visitors can experience St Lucia's hilly landscapes and the lush green of the rainforests on a trip in an open cable car. It floats though the treetops in the east of the island for 20 minutes. A guide then accompanies the visitor on a short walk that ends at the ziplines. From more than 45 m/150 ft up, you sail down seven spans on steel ropes for more than 1.5 m/0.9 mi – properly secured, of course.

SULPHUR SPRINGS AND DIAMOND FALLS

A worthwhile trip if you want to rent a car during your stay: the residents at Soufrières like to pilot visitors who arrive from Castries by the picturesque coastal road into the crater of a volcano you can drive onto (although not completely) with the words 'See the drive-in volcano'. You first have to park your car in the parking area *(daily 9am–5pm | EC$5/£1.43)*. Besides the *sulphur springs,* which announce their presence by the stink of sulphur, you can also visit the *Diamond Falls and Baths* for a relaxing bath. *Guided tours daily 10am–5pm | Sulphur Springs or Diamond Gardens EC$10/£2.86 each*

ST VINCENT

(⌁ 11/B2) **Besides St Vincent and the more southerly Grenadines, the Virgin**

BERTH

▶ ST LUCIA
From the cruise ship quay in Castries to the centre is about a 15-minute walk. Taxis are available in the port; negotiate the price before you take off.

Islands are regarded as the most beautiful sailing area of the Caribbean. The individual islands are often just a few kilometres apart in the bright, shallow turquoise water and delight not only sailors, but cruise ship passengers as well.

St Vincent (pop. 117,000) is an island of volcanic origin with corresponding vegetation, waterfalls and sulphur springs. Again, the British and the French fought about the islands in the 17th and 18th centuries. After the war against the 'Black Caribs', rebellious descendants of Caribs and slaves, which came to a bloody end in 1779, the British took possession of St Vincent. The island has been independent since 1979; however, the English queen is still the nominal head of state of the representative monarchy.

KINGSTOWN

With just 13,000 inhabitants, Kingstown is not only the capital, but also the island's largest city.

Founded by the French in 1722, the city was conquered by the British 57 years later. The port is an important economic factor; the island's agricultural products are shipped from here, and there are ferry connections to the neighbouring Grenadines.

BERTH

▶ **ST VINCENT**

In St Vincent cruise ships moor in the vicinity of the city centre. If you want to go touring in a taxi, negotiate a price before taking off.

SIGHTSEEING

BOTANICAL GARDENS ★

Kingstown's botanical garden, which was laid out in 1765, is the second oldest in the western hemisphere. Rare plants have been grown here since then; in addition, the *Nicholas Wildlife Aviary* breeds the rare St Vincent Amazon, a parrot species endemic to St Vincent and threatened with extinction. For about US$5/£3.8, you should get a guide to accompany you on your tour. *Daily 7am–6pm | Admission EC$5/£1.44 | Leeward Highway*

ST GEORGE'S CATHEDRAL

The present church, built in the early 19th century, stands on the site of its predecessor, which was destroyed by a hurricane in the late 18th century. With its battlements, the tower of the brightly painted church looks more like a tower of a fortification than that of a church. Inside, the colourful glass windows, which depict the crucifixion, among others, as well as the brass lectern with the unusual shape of an eagle, the mahogany pulpit and an artistically ornamented font cut from white marble are worth seeing. *Grenville Street | stgeorgescathedralsvg.com*

WHERE TO GO

INSIDER TIP **FALLS OF BALEINE**

The waterfall in the north-west is difficult to reach on foot. Rather join a boat tour, as offered by several operators. A picnic and a snorkelling break are included in the price of the ticket. *Boat tour: US$70–80/£54–62 per person*

FORT CHARLOTTE

The fortification complex rises 200 m/656 ft above the northern end of Kingstown bay. It was built in 1806 as a defence against attacks from the sea as well as by the 'Black Caribs' – many of the cannon are still pointed landward. The story of the Black Caribs is depicted in the rooms of the fort. *Mon–Fri 8am– 3pm| Admission US$2/£1.5 | Approx. 2.5 km/1.5 mi west of Kingstown*

GRENADA

(11/B3)* **The island (pop. 100,000) is a Caribbean idyll of a special kind owing to its varied landscapes and vegetation. Its volcano, Mount Qua Qua, is responsible for many of its natural attractions: rainforest, a crater lake and waterfalls are part of the large national park.**

The coast of the island of 311 km^2 /120 mi^2 is fringed by sandy beaches, mangrove thickets and steep slopes – interrupted here and there by the colourful little wooden houses of a sleepy fishing hollow. Coffee plantations, mango forests and bamboo groves extend up the low hills. The whole island smells of the exotic, because Grenada is the 'Spice Isle'; besides sugar cane, cacao and bananas, nutmeg, cloves, laurel, ginger, cinnamon, pimento and turmeric are grown here and exported all over the world. Grenada briefly grabbed the headlines in 1983 when a US invasion force occupied the island and overthrew the alleged communist government. The action was justified partly by the allegation that US students on the island were in danger and partly by the construction of a large airport with Cuban assistance. The US argued that this was an attempt by Castro to establish an air force base on the Lesser Antilles. After the 'aid mission', a provisional

Postcard idyll in the port of St George's

government was installed that soon held democratic elections. Grenada has since disentangled itself and recovered. Tourism, which had taken a severe blow, has picked up again.

ST GEORGE'S

Grenada's capital, they say, is the most beautiful of all Caribbean capitals. And so it is!

The houses of the city (pop. approx. 8000) extend up the hills in a semicircle around a bend and the natural harbour bay, called the Carenage. Down in the port one often sees the white cruise ships at anchor. But St George's is always abuzz with activity. On *Wharf Road* the small freighters that sail be-

GRENADA

The fascinating underwater sculpture park

tween the islands are loaded and un-loaded. And on the *Esplanade,* which faces the open sea, there's hustling and bustling.

GRENADA NATIONAL MUSEUM

Inside the building, which over the years has served as a barracks, prison, ho-tel and warehouse, one can marvel at, among others, the large copper boiler in which the sugar used to be boiled. *Mon–Fri 9am–4.30pm, Sat 10.30am–noon | Admission US$5/£3.88 | Young/Monckton St*

UNDERWATER SCULPTURES

Now who would have ever hit on that idea – exhibiting art under water! Well, the English diving instructor and artist Jason de Caires Taylor did, with his park of sculptures off the coast of Grenada, thereby creating an exciting hotspot for divers and snorkellers. There are

now more than 80 gypsum objects, which the marine inhabitants use as artificial reefs, thus creating a symbio-sis of art and nature. For the visitors to the park, it is an overwhelming experi-ence to see these figures lying, sitting or standing there, their appearance constantly changing with the current, light and sand.

WHERE TO GO

CONCORD FALLS ★

The three waterfalls near the town of Concord are worth a visit. For about 45 minutes, the road winds gently upward through nutmeg tree forests. It keeps crossing a small stream that feeds the lower falls. The climb itself is not very difficult, only the last few metres you have to clamber over large rocks in the riverbed. In the middle of the rainforest, the waterfall tumbles over a ledge into a pool 10 m/33 ft down. *On the coastal road from St George's to the town of Concord; from there the waterfalls are signposted | Admission US$1/£0.77*

DOUGALDSTON SPICE ESTATE

Grenada is known as the Spice Isle, and visitors notice this immediately when they arrive because the soft breeze sends the unmistakable aroma of exotic spices right up your nose. They are cultivated on a large scale here in plantations known as *spice estates*. Nutmeg in particular is sent all over the world, but cloves, cinnamon, laurel (bay), cacao, vanilla and saffron are also exported. Some plantations can be visited by means of guided tours, for example *Dougaldston Spice Estate.* Here you can learn a lot not only about cultivating, harvesting and processing, but your eyes and nose are also treated to a quite special sensory experience. *Gouyave, St John's | approx. 20 km/12.5 mi north of St George's*

GRAND ETANG

In the central highlands of the island, at an altitude of approx. 530 m/1740 ft and in the middle of the rainforest, lies the Grand Etang crater lake. This lake is now the centre of the national park. You can get information about the flora and fauna at the exhibition centre before you take a walk around the lake. *From St George's about halfway down the main road towards Grenville; the lake is signposted | Visitors' centre Sun–Fri 8am–4pm | Admission US$2/£1.5*

NUTMEG PROCESSING STATION

Here you can learn everything there is to know about this nut, the island's no. 1 export, and its flower, which is called mace. On guided tours, you visit the individual stations of the processing plant. The nuts are separated, dried, processed and packaged on three storeys and then shipped to the four corners of the earth. *Mon–Fri 10am–1pm and 2pm–4pm | Admission US$1/£0.75 | Central Depradine Street, Gouyave/St John*

RIVER ANTOINE RUM DISTILLERY ⊙

Since 1785 the method of producing the high-proof Grenada rum (organic quality!) has remained virtually unchanged. Even to this day the Antoine River drives the water wheel for the sugar cane press. When you sample the rum at the end of the tour, you should preferably choose the diluted rum punch – the original 75% rum is only for hard drinkers, and it ignites so easily that storing it on a cruise ship might not be a good idea. *Daily 9am–4pm | Admission US$2/£1.55 | River Antoine Estate | St Patrick's | Approx. 31 km/19.2 mi northeast of St George's*

BERTH

▶ GRENADA

In St George's cruise ships moor in the Melville Street Cruise Terminal. If there are many ships in port, ships at anchor may take their passengers ashore by tender. The bus terminal is about 500 m/550 yds from the cruise ship terminal. From here buses leave for different destinations on Grenada. Taxis and rental cars are also available. Note: If you want to drive a rental car, you need a local driver's licence!

BARBADOS

(𝄐 11/D2) **With a touch of pride in their voice, the residents call their island 'Little England'. And indeed, visitors will sense that the United Kingdom ruled here for centuries – and still does. Barbados is a constitutional monarchy, with the English queen at the head.**

Barbados is one of the few Caribbean islands whose economy is intact. Sugar and other sugar-cane products always were, and still are, a substantial part of imports and exports – the Mount Gay Rum from Barbados is one of the world's best. Barbados is not of volcanic origin, but simply a raised flat sheet of coral limestone. The capital city, Bridgetown, of which the suburbs transition into the extensive sugar-cane fields, lies in the south-west.

BRIDGETOWN

Bridgetown (pop. approx. 7000, excluding the suburbs) includes the old port, which is a widened extension of the mouth of the Constitution River.

The best place to start a stroll through the city is the port area. The old harbour basin is called The Careenage. It reminds of the times when the wooden sailing ships were pulled on land for repairs to the hull. This was called 'careening'. South of the Careenage lies the Waterfront Arcade, with some shops and restaurants. North of the Chamberlain bridge, which spans the river, are Trafalgar Square and the Houses of Parliament. in the south, behind the O'Neil bridge, the Fairchild Market is held every Saturday: a weekly Caribbean market that couldn't be noisier, more colourful and livelier.

To the west, The Wharf runs along the port; parallel to it, farther north, runs Broad Street, which is Bridgetown's main shopping street.

SIGHTSEEING

BARBADOS MUSEUM & HISTORICAL SOCIETY

Housed in a former military prison on Barbados, this museum documents much more than just the history of the island. There are ten exhibition sections covering, among others, the island's ecology, such as the coral reefs and the mangrove thickets, and its military history. *Mon–Sat 9am–5pm, Sun 2pm–6pm (closed on holidays) | St Ann's Garrison, St Michael | www.barbmuse.org.bb*

CRICKET MUSEUM

If you hadn't noticed it earlier, here the British influence becomes abundantly clear; after all, there is hardly any sport that is more British than cricket. And the British imported it into all their foreign territories, with considerable success. The Cricket Museum, appropriately located near the *Kensington Oval,* displays memorabilia and portraits of well-known Barbadian cricketers, and here are also a museum shop and a restaurant. *Mon–Fri 9.30am–5pm, Sat 9.30am–3pm | Fontabelle | www.cricketlegendsbarbados.com*

MOUNT GAY RUM VISITORS CENTRE

The history of the world's oldest rum unfolds in a 45-minute tour of the visitors' centre, although the actual production took place in the north of the island. You can watch a short film that explains the rum distillation process. Lastly, you can visit the warehouse

HIGH-GRADE WASTE

Taken with due care, rum – either neat or in a cocktail – is one of the culinary climaxes of a visit to the Caribbean. The liquor, which is made from molasses (a waste product of the cane pressing process) is the last evidence of the former dominance of sugar on the islands. Even today almost every island of the Lesser Antilles has its own brand, often even more than one, which makes it difficult to choose a personal favourite.

with countless barrels of rum, have a few samples or get yourself a bottle of the good stuff as a souvenir. *Mon–Fri 9am–4pm | Admission US$10/£7.82 | Spring Garden Highway | Brandons/ St Michael | Tel. 246 4 25 87 57 | www. mountgayrum.com*

TYROL COT HERITAGE VILLAGE
Gaily painted wooden *chattel houses,* where the workers used to live, surround the mansion built in 1854. Today they are shops selling local arts and crafts, from pottery to leather goods. *Mon–Fri 8am–4pm | Admission 10 BD$/£3.9 | Codrington Hill, St Michael*

WHERE TO GO

ANDROMEDA GARDENS ⭐
The small park complex houses a luxuriant abundance of tropical, subtropical and Mediterranean plants. In this huge garden there are two different circular paths that give you a good overview of the exotic plant world of the Caribbean and of many of the countries of this earth. Large trees cast the requisite shade, and the educational trails are well signposted. *Above Tent Bay | St Joseph | approx. 20 km/ 12.4 mi north-east of Bridgetown*

GUNHILL SIGNAL STATION ☼
A panoramic view of the island's hills as far as Bridgetown makes this tower, originally built for military purposes in the 18Th century, an impressive place to visit. *Mon–Sat 9am–5pm | Admission BD$10/£3.9 | Gun Hill | approx. 11 km/6.8 mi north-east of Bridgetown*

WELCHMAN HALL GULLY ⭐
The valley, a conservation area, is a treasure trove of Caribbean flora that stretches over 2 km/1.5 mi through limestone rocks. If you hear a rustle in the bush, it's a mongoose more likely than not. *Daily 9am–5pm | Admission BD$24/£9.4 | Off Highway 2 | St Thomas | approx. 15 km north-east of Bridgetown | www.welchmanhallgullybarbados.com*

BERTH

▶ **BARBADOS**
The modern cruise terminal is about 2 km/1.5 mi from the centre of Bridgetown. Taxis, rental cars and shuttle buses are available at the terminal. Negotiate the price with the taxi driver.

TRINIDAD AND TOBAGO

Trinidad is the larger of the two islands, and with an area of more than 4,800 km²/1850 mi² g it is in fact the largest in the Caribbean. Tobago, to the north, appears almost tiny by comparison; it covers barely 300 km²/116 mi².

Both islands, discovered by Columbus, have dream beaches – which is no surprise in the Caribbean. But they also have a rich plant and animal world, which (for good reasons) is specially protected, among others in the *Main Ridge Forest Reserve* on Tobago. More than 450 bird and more than 600 butterfly species flit through rainforests and savannahs; in the north of Trinidad, hidden in forests, lives the endemic Trinidad guan, a bird of the curassow family. The rare leatherback turtle, the largest of all turtles, can be found on Trinidad and Tobago. Seeing the gentle giants, which can tip the scales at more than 700 kg and whose carapace can grow to a length of more than 2 m/6 ft 6 in, come ashore to lay their eggs between March and August, is a special sight.

Besides beaches, the landscape features include mountain ranges – one on Tobago and three on Trinidad; the northernmost range, the Northern Range, has the island state's highest peak, Cerro del Aripo (940 m/4,600 ft). Unlike most of the Caribbean islands, neither Trinidad nor Tobago is of volcanic or coralline origin; they are thought to have broken off the mainland and share a number of physical features with Venezuela (which is just 11 km/7 mi from Trinidad and 34 km/21 from Tobago).

Photo: The carnival on Tinidad and Tobago is a riot of colour and vitality

One country, two islands: Trinidad and Tobago, the southernmost outliers of the Lesser Antilles, lie close to Venezuela

PORT OF SPAIN

(📖 11/B4) **The capital city of Trinidad and Tobago, Port of Spain, which with 50,000 inhabitants is one of the three largest cities of the island state, lies on the western foothills of the mountain range, at the Gulf of Paria.**

It is the economic centre of Trinidad and Tobago, with an important harbour where not only cruise ships moor, but from which cacao and asphalt are also exported worldwide.

While people were already living in the area of the present Port of Spain in the 16th century, the city only gained importance after the mid-18th century, when it became the seat of government. Today Port of Spain is a varied mixture of old and new; you will find buildings in the colonial style here, from the times of British rule, as well as modern features.

A RIOT OF COLOUR

It's well known that the Brazilians celebrate their carnival passionately. But the inhabitants of Trinidad and Tobago are also swept up in a collective trance every year when, with elaborate costumes and parades, their carnival is about to erupt in a blaze of colour. The festival follows a set rhythm: on carnival Monday, it kicks off at 4 in the morning (called *J'Ouvert*), then it's followed by two days of ecstatic celebrating, when thousands of people in colourful costumes move through the streets. And then there are the competitions: in the *Panorama* on carnival Saturday, steel bands perform in a musical competition, and in the *Kings and Queens Costume Competition* the year's best costumes are announced in the Queens Park Savannah.

The *Queen's Park Savannah*, formerly a French plantation of 10 ha, is now an enormous green on which not only horse races take place, but also open-air concerts and, of course, the carnival parades. area of 38 ha. Some 700 trees cast their shade in the tropical climate, between which carefully planned paths entice you to stroll around. *Daily 6am–6pm | Circular Road*

SIGHTSEEING

BOTANICAL GARDENS
The botanical garden, laid out in the early 19th century, is one of the oldest in the Caribbean and extends over an

The brightly coloured rufous-crested coquette belongs to the hummingbird family

EMPEROR VALLEY ZOO
The island state's only zoo lies directly next to the Queen's Park Savannah. Here you will see not only indigenous animals, but giraffes and tigers as well. *Daily 9am–6pm | Admission TT$30/£3.5 | Zoo Road*

MAGNIFICENT SEVEN
Immediately next to the Queen's Park Savannah, on the eastern side, there are seven imposing buildings built in the early 20th century. They all bear witness to the wealth of their owners, among whom there were two cacao plantation owners, the archbishop of Port of Spain and a doctor. Allow the fine and sometimes expensive details of the buildings, such as little towers, delicately crafted balconies and historicising elements of *Stollmeyer's Castle, Whitehall, Archbishop's Palace, Rommer, Mille Fleurs, Hayes Court* and the *Queen's Royal College* to sink in. *Maraval Road*

NATIONAL MUSEUM AND ART GALLERY

The museum, built to celebrate the diamond jubilee of Queen Victoria's coronation and therefore also known as the Royal Victoria Institute, contains not only exhibits concerning the greatest festive event of the islands, the carnival, but also artefacts from the era of the first inhabitants of the islands as well as a collection of national and international works of art. A branch of the museum is housed in Fort San Andres *(Tue–Fri 9am–15pm)*, a former fortress that offers a ☀ fine view of the green, forested hills *Tue–Sat 10am–6pm, Sun 2–5pm | Free admission | 117 Frederick Street*

WHERE TO GO

CARONI BIRD SANCTUARY

The *Caroni Swamp* covers 6000 ha south of Port of Spain. In the mangrove swamps, which are cut by watercourses, there are numerous bird species, including the scarlet ibis, a brilliantly orange-red bird with a long beak, which, together with Tobago's chachalaca, is the national bird of Trinidad and Tobago. Seeing large flocks of these birds skimming across the water in the evening is an impressive sight. Boat tours into the swamps depart from the visitors' centre; one of the operators is Nanan Bird Tours, which offers excursions of two and a half hours at 4pm every day / *www.nananecotours.com*

FORT GEORGE

West of Port of Spain lies the old fort the British built early in the 19th century for protection. In the 1880s the white signal house was built, from where signals were sent with flags to communicate the movements of ships.

Today there is a small museum in the house telling the history of the fort. Some of the cannon are on display, but the way to the fort is already worth it for the ☀ fantastic view of the capital below and the sea.

LA BREA PITCH LAKE

You probably know asphalt for its use to surface roads and do not associate it with any kind of natural phenomenon. On Trinidad you can also experience it as a lake – pay a visit to the La Brea Pitch Lake, the world's largest occurrence of asphalt, approx. 86 km/53.5 mi south of Port of Spain. At the end of the 19th century, mining asphalt became an important part of Trinidad's economy; today the lake, in which you can actually swim, attracts crowds of visitors.

MARACAS BAY

Beach fans shouldn't miss it – Maracas Bay has no less than three dream beaches: Las Cuevas, Maracas and Tyrico Beach, with the requisite infrastructure. *Approx. 23 km/14.2 mi north-east of Port of Spain*

BERTH

▶ TRINIDAD AND TOBAGO

In Trinidad, cruise ships moor at the Port of Spain Cruise Ship Complex. From here you can get to the centre on foot in about 25 minutes. Taxis are available at the port (negotiate the price beforehand and find out whether payment must be in US or Trinidad dollars), as are maxitaxis, which run on defined routes.

ABC-ISLANDS

Just off the Venezuelan coast lies a group of islands that used to belong to the Dutch Antilles, is now considered part of the Lesser Antilles and is called the ABC islands: Aruba, Bonaire and Curaçao.

They are all colourful and friendly, but they offer visitors totally different experiences. Aruba, the smallest of the three sisters, has the prettiest beaches. The submarine world of Bonaires is a nature paradise, with intact coral reefs abounding with exotic, flashy fishes. The largest of the three islands, Curaçao, offers cosmopolitan flair and much culture. The colourful houses of Willemstad, the capital city, still reflects the heritage from the colonial period. And its classification as a

World Cultural Heritage site by Unesco is something very unusual in this part of the world. The fact that all three islands are relatively dry is not only reflected in the desert-like scenery of the countryside, but also has the benefit that you do not constantly have to deal with tropical downpours.

ARUBA

(⌕ 12/A-B2) **Air and water temperatures of 27 and 26 °C are almost the same on the small Caribbean island of Aruba. It's perfect bathing weather for those looking forward to a great swimming experience during their cruise – and the cherry on top is 12 km/**

Photo: In Oranjestad the colonial style blends with the vivid colours of the Caribbean

The names pragmatically abbreviated, the nature a dream full of colours and impressions – the three islands in a nutshell

7.5 mi of absolutely beautiful beaches of perfect sand.

Eagle Beach, on the north-western coast, is particularly popular with tourists; palms sway in the breeze and palm frond sunscreens provide the shade. Besides the beaches and the fantastic submarine world, there is also an interesting landscape with enormous cacti, aloe veras and divi-divi trees bent by the wind to explore. The Arikok national park occupies one fifth of the island's surface, and among other things you can see Indian caves with rock paintings which are more than 1000 years old. The history of the island was shaped by many cultures, and many more influences can be found besides those of the Dutch colonial period. Today people of about 90 nationalities live on the island, which has a population of more than 120,000.

ORANJESTAD

With a name like Oranjestad, one would expect Aruba's little capital to be Dutch

through and through; yet you will find an incomparable blend of Dutch-Caribbean flair here.

Since 2013, an open tramway connects the port with the pedestrian zone, where you can admire the gingerbread buildings, painted in soft pastel colours, from the colonial period. Here visitors will find a range of international boutiques, art galleries and jewellery shops, as well as a great number of restaurants and pavement cafés. Between

ago are exhibited in a very modern way and with the latest technology, including interactivity. You can immerse yourself in Aruba's Indian heritage, represented by handicrafts, ceramics, spiritual objects and other artefacts of Amerindian culture. There are regular guided tours, and the museum has an English-speaking guide on hand. Inquisitive visitors to the museum can enjoy a restorative in the museum's cafeteria. *Schelpstraat 42*

Blue sea as far as the eye can see: view from the California Lighthouse

the city lagoon and the Paardenbaai (Horse Bay), a fabulous park stretches along the waterfront.

SIGHTSEEING

ARCHAEOLOGICAL MUSEUM AND STORE

This museum, covering 1700 m^2/2033 yds^2, was built in 2009 in a complex of historical buildings. The valuable artefacts from more than 5000 years

INSIDER TIP ARUBA ALOE FACTORY MUSEUM AND STORE

One of the most fascinating medicinal plants is the aloe vera, which is cultivated in Aruba. Despite its relatively unspectacular appearance, it possesses remarkable properties that help people heal wounds or moisturise the skin. This is particularly beneficial after a generous dose of Caribbean sunshine. Help is at hand in the products that have been manufactured in, for example, the *Aloe Factory* in Hato, just outside Oranjestad, since 1890. You can join a guided tour through the adjacent museum of the factory; tours start every 15 minutes. *115 Pita St.*

FORT ZOUTMAN ⭐

Fort Zoutman is one of Oranjestad's oldest buildings, around which the town developed at the end of the 18th century. Next to it, the conspicu-

ous Willem III tower was built in 1866, intended to serve as a beacon and the official clock tower. After its restoration it was used to set up Aruba's museum, where the exhibits cover the evolution of the city and various other themes. Tuesday is a good day for a visit, because at 6pm the inner court opens for a market with arts and crafts, culinary specialities and historic dances in traditional costumes. *Zoutmanstraat 6*

WHERE TO GO

ALTO-VISTA-CHAPEL

The small chapel, standing completely by itself on the hills of Aruba about 11 km/6.8 mi north of Oranjestad, is worth the trip. The perky little building dates back to 1952, but a church was already built here in 1750 that gradually fell into disrepair. The chapel has now again become a destination for pilgrims – for Christians and for tourists. Mass is celebrated once a week, but the church is open every day. 'Alto Vista' means 'high view', and from here you can indeed 🔆 see the whole island.

CALIFORNIA LIGHTHOUSE

On the coast, approximately 17 km/10.5 mi from Oranjestad, you will find the California Lighthouse, 55 m/180.5 ft high. It is on the northernmost tip of the island, on Arashi Beach. It is called after the American steamship 'California', which ran aground here in 1891 and is still a popular spot for wreck divers. The tower was completed in 1916 to warn ships of the dangerous shallows at the island. Its slender, bright looks make it a photogenic object against the blue sky.

BERTH

▶ ARUBA

The port of Oranjestad has five modern terminals, allowing several cruise ships to moor simultaneously. The centre can be reached on foot; for excursions into the surroundings, taxis, rental cars and a number of operators are available in the port.

You can't go inside, but what used to be the lighthouse keeper's bungalow is now occupied by an Italian restaurant where you can take five and enjoy the sunset.

BONAIRE

(*12/D2*) **Bonaire is the second largest of the ABC islands. Its submarine world, known as outstanding, comprises coral reefs that are still fully intact and frequented by colourful schools of tropical fishes.**

In order to keep them pristine, a large part of the sea is a protected marine reserve where fishing on the reef is prohibited and large boats are not allowed to

WHITE GOLD

What first attracted the Dutch at the time lies in the south of Bonaire: natural salt lakes, which were developed into profitable salt pans. The high-quality salt from the sea is formed here by simple evaporation in the large evaporation ponds, which are still being operated. For the people, this is an economic factor, and for many flamingos it offers an excellent habitat. What one also sees besides the ponds glittering in various colours and the characteristic white, shining kilometres of salt mounds, are the small stone huts built during the colonial period for the slaves who in those days cleaned the flats and recovered the salt. They are now protected monuments.

anchor. The southern part of the island offers something very special: the salt lagoons of the Pekelmeer are home to swarms of flamingos that come here to feed in the shallow waters. The blinding white of the salt mounds, together with the pink plumage of the birds and the shining pink particles creates a brilliant play of colour.

KRALENDIJK

The colourful capital of Bonaire enchants visitors with its relaxed, Caribbean charm, which is permeated with relics from the Dutch colonial period. As it is easy to get an overall view of the city (pop. 12,000), it's best to explore it on foot. The snug little houses, painted in different colours and with small gardens, date back to the 18th and 19th centuries, when the Dutch were still the colonial masters here. Traditionally, the ground floor housed a shop, and the living quarters were on the first floor. Now you find many souvenir shops here, boutiques and nice cafés. In the port many boats are at anchor, and near the pier you will find an open hall where the fish market has been located since 1935.

SIGHTSEEING

FORT ORANJE ★
The orange-tinted fort is on the coastal road, and from 1639 it was used by the Dutch East India Company to protect the port of Bonaire. It is the city's oldest building. From the 19th century, the settlement of Kralendijk ('coral dike') developed around it. In 1932 a lighthouse was added, which still rises in the middle of the fort. It is surrounded by some British cannons, because the English subsequently conquered the island. Today objects from the history of Bonaire are

The submarine world around the ABC islands is uniquely colourful

exhibited here. There is no official tour, but you can stroll around and read the display boards. *Kaya C.E.B. Hellmund*

TERRAMAR MUSEUM

Kralendijk's historical and archaeological museum lies in the centre of the city. A visit takes you back up to 7000 years into the past of the Caribbean islands. The early Amerindian occupation, the times of exploitation and the colonial era are illustrated. To this end the museum makes use of valuable artefacts, 3D reconstructions as well as interactive exhibits such as video projections. There are also interesting special exhibitions at regular intervals. Guided tours take one hour and are presented in English too. *Kaya J.N.E. Craane 6*

TIME CAPSULE

If you stroll down the *Kaya Grandi*, Kralendijk's prettiest shopping street, you will see a blue-white, sarcophagus-like stone structure. The time capsule, as it is called, was set up here and outfitted by the local Lions Club. Inside the capsule there is a container with objects from actual life at present, such as a CD, PC, mobile phone or pocket calculator. A report describing current affairs of that year was written, and there are letters from people who want to address people in the future, for the capsule will only be opened after 40 years – on February 2, 2042.

BERTH

▶ BONAIRE

In Kralendijk, cruise ships moor right in the centre. Taxis and shuttle rental cars are available at the port.

SPECIALITIES

The Caribbean is a melting pot of nations, so it's small wonder that in the kitchen the most diverse influences play out and that the palate is treated to a delicious patchwork. In fact, each island also has its own indigenous dishes, which are full of surprises. These include, among others, the *Sopi de Bananas*, cooked bananas in soup, the fried fish balls called *bitterbai*, pea soup with meat and sausage *(erwtensoep)*, the *Sanger Yena*, dark Aruban offal sausages and, probably very exotic for visitors but very popular among locals, the *iguana soup*.

CURAÇAO

(🗺 12/C2) **The letter C in the name ABC islands stands for Curaçao, which lies between Aruba and Bonaire. The largest of the three islands is a multicolour, happy experience.**

Candy-coloured houses mix with turquoise sea, white beaches, wild orchids and brightly coloured birds and patterned fishes. There's colour in the glasses too, because the famous Curaçao liqueur is manufactured here from bitter oranges and distributed all over the world. Although it's best known as crystal blue, the original drink has the colour of amber. It is now also available in red or green, and it's worth sampling right here where it's produced.

WILLEMSTAD

The capital city of the island of Curaçao seems to have been taken out of a Dutch picture book. Here one colourful house follows the next, and all are preserved in the colonial style.

You could almost believe you're in Amsterdam, with its canals and pavement cafés, if it were not for these candy colours and the incredibly fine weather. This mixture of Old European culture and Caribbean is an absolutely fascinating mixture that has earned the city the status of a Unesco World Heritage site. The historical centre is the work of Jewish settlers who arrived here with the West India Company via Amsterdam and settled here. Over and above the wonderful flair, Willemstad is also one of the best shopping spots of the Caribbean.

SIGHTSEEING

FORT AMSTERDAM
In Punda, which is touristically speaking the most attractive part of the town, the Dutch built Fort Amsterdam in 1634 to protect the port. The mighty fortress, built on a spit and shining like cream in the sunlight, has been listed by Unesco and still watches over the entry to the harbour. While it is not the only fort on the island, it is the fort visited most because it also has a church and a museum. It is also the residence of the Dutch governor. You will know he is there when the flag is up. The fort itself is not open to the public, as it is the seat of government, but the Protestant church with its museum is a little gem and well worth a visit. A special feature there is a cistern with crystal-clear water.

FORT RIF
Right opposite Fort Amsterdam, in the

bewitching suburb of Otrabanda, stands Fort Rif. It was built in 1828 to protect this quarter and to support the third fort, the Water Fort. However, after its completion it already no longer served any purpose, and early in the 20th century large parts were torn down. Today the perfectly renovated remains are used for a different purpose. A shopping mall has moved in which, besides the branches of many

times they were also used by escaped slaves as a hideout. Visitors can see only a part of the cave on foot, but even on this limited route the appearance and shapes of the dripstones are impressive. You will also see shining basins of water and small waterfalls, and there's also a colony of long-nosed dogs living there. At the entrance to the caves there is a small bar.

The Netherlands in Caribbean guise in Willemstad

international chains, also has a casino and some restaurants and bars with live music. *Baden Powel Road 1, Otrabanda*

HATO CAVE

The Hato cave was formed under water millions of years ago, before Curaçao rose from the deep. The cave system, covering some 4900 m² /4860 yds², contains a large number of impressive limestone formations, and on the walls there are prehistoric murals. The caves were of cultic significance to the original inhabitants of the island, but in colonial

BERTH

▶ CURAÇAO

Willemstad has several cruise ship piers, some of which can also accommodate the largest ships. The town centre can be reached on foot. Taxis and rental cars are available for trips on the islands.

TRAVEL TIPS

GENERAL

The U.S. Virgin Islands, for instance, offers an entirely different cultural experience than the nearby British Virgin Islands or the French island of Guadeloupe, so depending on where you go and which country currently or formerly occupies the island you're visiting, you'll have a uniquely different time.

HEALTH

No inoculations are required. Nevertheless, a combined shot for hepatitis and tetanus is recommended. Medical care varies from one island to the next. Basically, you are well looked after; in more serious cases you will be taken from a small island to the next larger island with a hospital by helicopter. In the southern Caribbean, chikungunya fever occurs, which is caused by a mosquito-borne virus; it is usually harmless, but characterised by severe pain in the joints. Do take out international health insurance and take along a well-planned emergency kit as well as a high-factor sunscreen lotion.

INTERNET & WIFI

In the Caribbean, the internet is available wherever international business is done; hotels, charter companies, water sport and diving enterprises, tourist bureaus etc. usually have their own websites. Emails can be sent from many post offices. WiFi hotspots can be found everywhere on the Lesser Antilles.

LANGUAGE

Avoid the sloppy US expression "Hi!" when saluting the locals. On the islands, it is customary (and polite) to be a little more formal and say good morning, good day, good afternoon, good evening and (after 7pm) good night.

MONEY & CURRENCY

On most of the islands of the Lesser Antilles, payment is made in East Caribbean dollars (EC$), but the US$ is also readily accepted. Exceptions are the Virgin Islands (US$), the French islands (euros), the Dutch islands (Antillen guilder, NAf) and Barbados (Barbadian dollar, BD$). Travellers' cheques are a convenient and safe means of payment. Credit cards of the large international organisations are now also accepted. Some banks have ATMs where you can use European cards.

ON THE ROAD

Except on the Dutch and French islands, traffic keeps to the left. Nevertheless, on the Virgin Islands the cars are left-hand drive. If you want to go on tour in a rented car, note the following: on curves with a poor view it is customary to hoot as a warning to oncoming traffic. Drive slowly and carefully. Heavy downpours and storms regularly open up potholes or blow obstacles onto the road, and animals may cross the road at any time.

Lesser Antilles

**Your holiday from start to finish:
the main information for your trip**

PHOTOGRAPHY

Before you photograph a local or his house, you should ask them if it's OK. The inhabitants of most of the islands generally do not react as aggressively to this request as on Jamaica, for example, but it is still regarded as impolite to take snapshots of unknown people without asking.

POST

Air mail is usually transported within one week; everything else can take several weeks. Post offices are open in the mornings and main post offices in the afternoon as well.

SAFETY

Except for the US Virgin Islands, the Lesser Antilles are among the safest holiday destinations. Most of the locals lock neither their front door nor their car. Nevertheless, it is best not to leave valuables on the beach in full view, of course.

TAXI

There are enough taxis on all the islands. Have the correct amount on hand. Collective travel is a cheap alternative. In the francophone parts, it is called *public* or *tap tap*, on the anglophone islands jitney, cab or bus. You pay individually.

TELEPHONE & MOBILE PHONE

Telephone calls are by satellite, and communication is excellent. A call to Central Europe costs about US$3 per minute. Each island sells its own telephone card, which can be used at any public phone (usually at the post office). The code for England is 00 44. The country code for the Antilles is 001 followed by the respective island code. Few mobile providers have roaming contracts with the Lesser Antilles. Ask your provider about the costs.

TIPPING

In food outlets, a service charge is often already indicated on the bill. Otherwise 10–15 % is normal. Also in the case of (often self-appointed) tour guides, don't be too parsimonious.

UNITS OF MEASUREMENT

Besides the English units such as miles and pounds, the use of kilometres and kilos is gaining ground. 1 mile = 1.609 km.

BUDGETING

Rum	$9 / £7	*for a bottle of Mount Gay rum*
Breakfast	$7.50–10 / £6–8	*for a sandwich/burger*
Cocktail	$6.70–11 / £5.30–8.80	*In a restaurant/bar*
Bus trip	$1.10 / £0.90	*for a bus ticket*

MEXICO

A coastline of more than 12,000 km/ 7500 mi – that sounds like a lot, and that it is. Part of Mexico's fascinating coastline is best explored by cruising and diving into a country that offers much more than world-famous beaches such as Acapulco and numerous small, secret bays you can go and swim in.

For instance, on the Yucatán peninsula in southern Mexico: here the classical Maya culture comes to life. The ancestors of the present Maya venerated an invisible world that was nonetheless present. Their priests turned it into a second reality through rites and mental inner vision. For many centuries, the Pacific coast in the west of the country was populated by just a few fishers; it was the hunting ground of pirates who plundered the ships, loaded with gold and silver, of the Spanish colonial power. Today there are many holiday destinations on this curvaceous coast that attract a multitude of visitors. Well-known seaside resorts alternate with peaceful bays, and lagoons are home to numerous aquatic birds.

COZUMEL

(🔯 14/D3) **The producer of submarine films Jacques-Yves Cousteau turned the small Caribbean islands into an internationally famed diver's paradise.**

These days more than half the visitors come here to dive. Most of them go to

About 25,000 archaeological sites, stylish colonial buildings and a bountiful nature: that, and much more, is Mexico

the Palancar reef, but the submarine caves off the Chankanaab lagoon are also known for their tropical flora and fauna. The lively island 20 km/12.5 mi off the eastern coast of Yucatán and about 50 x 15 km/31 x 9 mi in size also attracts many visitors from cruise ships in winter who explore the small island capital of San Miguel de Cozumel. However, if possible you should not leave it at that, because the surroundings also offer many other destinations worth seeing.

ARRECIVE PALANCAR (PALANCAR REEF)

You have a little spare time, and moreover enjoy diving and snorkelling? Then you should not pass up this coral reef. It extends over a length of 5 km on the south-western coast of Cozumel and is characterised by caves and steep walls. The fascinating submarine world is home to schools of rare fish species and enormous turtles. The Palancar reef, a dorado

WILD WHIRLIES

The pre-Columbian Caribbean god Huracán gave the whirlwind its name. In the autumn of each year it's that time again, when masses of air with different temperatures and humidity collide over the Caribbean. Then the storms rage across the sea and the islands towards the coast at speeds up to 200 km/h. Fortunately hurricanes can mostly be predicted, so that people are not normally hurt.

sunken figure of Our Lady of Guadalupe. Add a park-like landscape with a botanical garden, as well as numerous reconstructions of the country's most significant pre-Columbian sites, buildings and sculptures. The lagoon, which has a subterranean connection with the sea, hosts numerous fishes and birds, and a small marine museum presents a view of the underwater world. Restaurants and bars sell tacos and *bocadillos* for a few pesos. Note, however, that this ideal snorkelling place for beginners always attracts many visitors. *Mon–Sat 8am–4pm| Costera Sur km 11 | 21 US$/£16,5 | www. cozumelparks.com*

for experienced divers, lies about 8 m below the surface. It is divided into several parts. The Maracaibo reef drops down to far beyond 30 m and is renowned for its spectacular coral formations. You reach the best diving and snorkelling areas by boat. *Deep Blue (Calle Salas 200 | Tel. 01987 8 72 56 53 | deepbluecozumel. com)* is a reputable address for divers and a member of the National Association of Underwater Instructors (NAUI). Never learnt to dive? Parrotfish, damselfish and bizarre coral formations can also be observed on snorkelling trips – also a fabulous experience in the crystal clear 30 °C water.

CHANKANAAB BEACH ADVENTURE PARK

The nature reserve on Cozumel's west coast promises to deliver a relaxing day at the seaside, complete with the obligatory infrastructure. A plus for divers and snorkellers is a coral reef between 7 and 30 m deep right off the beach where, to the delight of the devout Mexicans, there is a INSIDER TIP ▶

MUSEO DE LA ISLA DE COZUMEL

The museum displays excavated finds from the pre-Columbian era, some of which were salvaged from the sea by divers. The arrival of the Spanish conquerors Hernán Cortés and Juan Grijalva in the 16th century marked a turning point for Cozumel as well. The island became a base for pirates and freebooters – some of the museum exhibits demonstrate this graphically. An exhibition that will also interest children shows Cozumel's coral reefs and their rare denizens. *Mon–Sat 9am–4pm | Av. Rafael Melgar/6a Calle*

PLAYA Y PARQUE ECOTURÍSTICO PUNTA 🌾

From the Visitors' Center, the double-decker bus bounces along through the reserve (crocodiles, tortoises, birds) to the lighthouse. A 2 km/1.5 mi beach runs around the park, and a coral reef invites you to come snorkelling. The white lighthouse (133 steps) from 1901 on the southern tip gives you a 360° view over the southern part of Cozumel and the Caribbean sea. The former living quarters of the keeper at its foot have been converted into a small INSIDER TIP maritime museum. *Mon– Sat 9am–4pm | Admission 14 US$/£11 | Costera Sur km 27 | www.cozumelparks.com*

SAN GERVASIO

The spiritual centre of Cozumel: a thousand years ago, Mayan women from Belize, Guatemala and the south of Mexico went on pilgrimages to the island to pay homage to Ix-Chel, the goddess of the moon and of fertility, in San Gervasio on the island. To the fortunate women, the goddess revealed herself in their dreams as an old woman with clawed feet and snakes with flickering tongues around her head or as a laughing, pretty young girl and promised to help the dreamer fulfil her dreams. San Gervasio is still venerated by the Mayas as a holy place of power. Externally, there is little to see – between dense shrubs and palms lie some decaying arches, temple ruins and the remains of an ancient ceremo-

nial path – still, it's worth coming here: it is said that if they sit quite still and close their eyes, sensitive people have a very special, powerful experience. *Daily 8am–4.30pm| 10 km/6.2 mi east of San San Miguel*

FOOD & DRINK

EL ABUELO GERARDO

Authentic Mexican cuisine, rare on Cozumel, speciality: fish dishes. The seats on the patio are very popular. *San Miguel | 10a Av. 21 (opposite the San Miguel church) | Tel. 01987 8 72 10 12 |Moderate*

INSIDER TIP RESTAURANTE DEL MUSEO ☼

This café-restaurant is recommended not only after a museum visit. It is on the first floor and has a large terrace facing the sea from where you can watch the passing parade on the main street. *Permanently open Mon-Sat. San Miguel | Av. Rafael Melgar/4aCalle|Tel. 019871202255 | Budget*

San Gervasio, a holy Maya site and place of power: San Gervasio

MÉRIDA

(🕮 14/A2) **The wealthy colonial city is the capital as well as the economic and cultural centre of the Free and Sovereign State of Yucatán.**

Nowhere else will you see so many beautifully restored city palaces – between 1880 and 1920, the sisal trade grew the city into one of the world's richest metropolises (pop. 1.3 million) – and so many beautiful avenues, patios and arcades. Many historical buildings now accommodate hotels, restaurants and museums.

INSIDER TIP On weekends, the centre is traffic free; on Saturdays for the street festival *El Corazón de Mérida*, with much music and dancing, and on Sundays it continues with street vendors, music, processions and open-air restaurants. While on the one side of the square the trumpets of a *mariachi* band and the plaintive songs of tragicomic macho singers about love and sorrow bring tears to the eyes of the listeners, some Mayas play softly on the marimba, an instrument similar to a xylophone. In between children run about, balloon and ice-cream vendors tout their treasures, people enjoy enchiladas and candy floss.

SIGHTSEEING

GRAN MUSEO DEL MUNDO MAYA ★
There's no way around it: the museum just outside the city centre is world class. Take a good look and you will see that the hypermodern structure imitates the branches and leaves of the ceiba tree, which the Maya considered holy. Do allow yourself a few hours: the magnificent, imaginative conception of the halls, the exhibits (more than 1000!), short films and presentations are captivating – partly because they centre around today's Mayas. Besides an exhibition of bewitching Maya clothing, the hall contains old-fashioned kitchenware and toys, which the Maya still make themselves today. Other halls focus on cults and rites, among other things. Fascinating detail: the descriptions are not only in Spanish and English, but also INSIDER TIP in the language of the Mayas. *Wed–Mon 8am–5pm | Calle 60 Norte 299e | www.granmuseodelmundomaya.com.mx*

MUSEO DE ANTROPOLOGÍA ★
Finds from the prehistoric period as well as from the different eras of the pre-Columbian Maya culture: ceramics, stelae, sculptures, burial gifts and jewellery, all exhibited in a beautiful palace of the early 20th century that briefly served as the residence of general Cantón Rosado, one of the most influential inhabitants of the city. A particularly appealing feature of the city is the meeting between the vain splendour of colonial architecture and the archaic-looking shapes of the items exhibited, which are inspirational because of their simplicity and reduced aesthetics. *Tue–Sun 8am–5pm | Paseo de Montejo/Calle 43*

MUSEO DE ARTE POPULAR
You won't find a more beautiful collection of Yucatec popular art anywhere on the peninsula. Besides sisal products, baskets and hammocks there are, for example, also hand-painted papermaché dolls, costumes and handicrafts from other Mexican states. At the sales office, there are many products you can buy for just a few pesos. *Tue-Sat 10am–5pm, Sun 10am–3pm | Calle 59 no. 441*

PALACIO DEL GOBIERNO
The government palace has several *murales* (murals) by Fernando Castro Pa-

checo. A famous painting is the gigantic 'Hands of the Henequén labourer' in the naturalist style, an indication of the almost slave-like working conditions of the plantation workers in earlier days. From the 🌿 palace balconies, you can enjoy an outstanding view of the cathedral square. *Daily 8am–8pm | Northern side of the Plaza Mayor*

TURIBÚS 🌿

An open double-decker bus runs from Zócalo to the main attractions of the city every 45 minutes; you can get on or off at seven stops. *Daily 9am–9pm | Duration 1¾ h | 120 pesos/£5 | turibusmerida.com*

WHERE TO GO

DZIBILCHALTÚN

One of the oldest and largest Maya sites lies approx. 20 km/12.5 mi north of Mérida. Dzibilchaltún ('writing on flat stone') dates from the pre-classical era and was still inhabited when the Spaniards arrived here. The extensive complex, comprising a substantial number of structures (about 8400) covered 16 km²/6 mi², but only the large centre (3 km²/1.2 mi²) has been excavated. Inside the complex 12 *sacbeob* were discovered – 15 m wide paved streets, up to 1 km long, most of them leading to the centre. From this Plaza Mayor a sacbé of 425 m runs to the brilliantly restored *templo* (or *pirámide) de las Siete Muñecas* ('of the seven dolls'). The seven small clay figures found on an altar here are now in Mérida's archaeological museum.

PROGRESO

Yucatán's most important port (pop. 56,000), where cruise ships also moor, lies 36 km north of Mérida. It was completed in 1856 for exporting sisal and thrived on it. The pier, 2 km/1.5 mi long and 9 m wide, seems to extend endlessly from the white beach through the shallow water and into the sea. Large ships can even berth 6.5 km/4 mi off the coast, because a further 4.5 km/2.8 mi viaduct runs from the pier to the deep-sea harbour. Numerous open-air restaurants and cafés line the long beach promenade. Here the inhabitants of Méridas love to spend a couple of quiet days off, and if you like you can also indulge in the holiday atmosphere.

One of the many historical buildings of Mérida, the Casa Consistorial

The daredevil cliff jumpers of Acapulco

ACAPULCO

(🛱 15/F4) **Hotels, restaurants and discotheques line the glittering bay on Mexico's west coast, million-dollar dream villas nestle on the hill of Las Brisas.**

Cruise liners berth in the old harbour, while street vendors and *mariachis* are characteristic of the Zócalo. And let's not forget the kilometres of sandy beaches that made Acapulco (pop. 2 million) the coastal resort and playground of well-heeled US Americans in the 1940s.

SIGHTSEEING

CLIFF JUMPERS ⭐ ⌇

The *clavadistas*, who dive spectacularly from the 42 m high Quebrada rock into a narrow inlet head first and can be seen on countless Acapulco posters, can be watched live every day. The best view of the floodlit scenery is from the terraces of the restaurant *La Perla (in the Hotel Mirador | Tel. 01744 4 83 11 55 | Expensive)*; you won't get a better view anywhere. *Special exhibition daily 7.30, 8.30, 9.30, 10.30pm as well as 12.45am | On the western edge of the Old Town*

FUERTE DE SAN DIEGO ⌇

Bastions several metres thick and a dream view of the sea characterise the 18th-century fort that protected Acapulco against pirate attacks. Today it fascinates visitors as a historical museum, recalling the colonial times when Acapulco's port was (almost) the navel of the world. T*ue 9.30am–6.30pm| Calle Hornitos off Costera M. Alemán*

FOOD & DRINK

INSIDER TIP LA CABAÑA DE CALETA

The beach restaurant in an open *palapa* scores with its large and Inexpensive assortment of seafood, to be enjoyed with a great view of bathers and fishing boats. *Fraccionamiento Las Playas | Playa Caleta Oriente | Tel. 01744 4 69 85 53 | www. lacabanadecaleta.com | Moderate*

ZIBU ⌇

You can bet on it: the Thai-Mexican fusion food will bowl you over, and this is one of Acapulco's top addresses. Tropical-romantic atmosphere high above the *Bahía de Puerto Marqués*. Small, variable menu with delicious desserts. *Frac-*

cionamiento Glomar | Avenida Escénica | Tel. 01744 4 33 30 69 | www.zibu.com.mx | *Expensive*

MANZANILLO

(□ 15/B2) **Manzanillo (pop. 130,000), on Mexico's west coast, is important especially because of its port, which is Mexico's largest freight harbour, but also accommodates cruise ships.**

Manzanillo has several fine beaches, such as the *Playa Azul* and the *Playa Las Brisas*, which shimmer like gold in the tropical sunlight – and they do this almost all year round. In the hinterland rise the dense, green, tropical forests in charming contrast with the sea and sand. On Manzanilla's beach promenade, in the comprehensively renovated city centre, the enormous blue sculpture of a sailfish by the Mexican artist Sebastian catches the eye.

SIGHTSEEING

IGUANARIO ARCHUNDIA

Saving and preserving iguanas is what Ramón Medina Archundia has dedicated himself to here in the centre of Manzanillo, where he lovingly cares for the reptiles. Especially for children, seeing these animals that resemble little dragons is quite an experience. *Daily 10am–6pm | 21 de marzo #521 | Admission: donation expected www.facebook.com/Iguanario Manzanillo*

OLA BRISA GARDENS

In this "civilised jungle", as they call it themselves, you plunge into the opulent nature of western Mexico with hundreds of different palms and tropical plants. *Guided tours Mon–Sat 9 or 9.30am (sign up under olabrisagardens@gmail.com) | Tel.31433-0856 | Prolongacion Arnulfo Flores#7 | Santiago (Manzanillo) | olabrisagardens.com*

WHERE TO GO

EL TORTUGARIO

In the rescue centre El Tortugario in Cuyutlán, approx. 43 km/26.7 mi east of Manzanillo, the marine turtles threatened with extinction find a temporary home before they are released back into freedom. The activities of the ecology centre now also include iguanas and crocodiles. *Daily except Wednesdays 9am–5pm | Av. Lopez Mateo, 28350 Cuyutlán | Admission 40 US$/£31.3 | tortugari ocuyutlan.com*

LOVE SONG, ANYONE?

The *mariachi* bands, these honourable gentlemen in their proud habit of black suits with shining golden or silver buttons and wide sombreros, are the epitome of Mexican music. Up to ten musicians play bass, guitar, violin and trumpet, accompanying passionate singing. If the *mariachis* perform in restaurants, you owe them a *propina* (tip) if you ask for a specific song. If they offer their services on squares, you agree a commensurate compensation in advance (approx. 7–8 US$/£5.5–6.2 a song).

The symbol of Cabo San Lucas is the rock arch El Arco

PUERTO VALLARTA

(🗺 15/A1) **In the Bay of Banderas there are more than two dozen of golden beaches waiting for you.**

Despite the 2.5 million visitors a year, the atmosphere in the former fishing village on both sides of the Río Cuale (pop. 350,000) has remained typically Mexican: paved inner-city streets, red-tiled roofs and wrought-iron balconies dominate the urban landscape. Construction takes place in the north and on the coast. The high life is lived on the beaches. Besides the classical sports, there are trips into the jungle for the adventurous with an appetite for something different during their cruise.

SIGHTSEEING

ISLA DEL RÍO CUALE ★

The 5-ha island attracts visitors with wonderfully styled cafés and restaurants as well as way-out handicraft shops. It can be reached from both road bridges as well as by a pedestrian bridge near the mouth. On the park-like island, the streets lead through gardens densely vegetated with palms and bamboo, among others, to romantic spots. The roads are lined with handicraft stands and shops. A statue of John Huston reminds of Puerto Vallarta's cinematic history. There are neither cars nor noise, only quiet and shady roads.

LOS CABOS/ CABO SAN LUCAS

Where the Pacific and the Gulf of California meet, everything is designed for fun, recreation and action.

At the southern tip of the Baja California peninsula, which is 1550 km/963 mi long, the bundu makes room for innumerable luxury resorts, restaurants and clubs, the greens of costly golf courses. Outside the picture is totally different: the lonely, bizarre desert landscape with cardón cacti growing metres tall.

Los Cabos consists of two cities: the more peaceful San José del Cabo (pop. 70,000) and the party epicentre Cabo San Lucas (pop. 70,000), just more than 30 km to the south-west, where parties rock around the clock in the clubs and bars.

SIGHTSEEING

EL ARCO
The offshore rock formation with a natural arch on the side where the Pacific and the Gulf of California meet is the emblem of the city. You can see the arch from the mainland, and there are also boat trips from the harbour.

FARO DE CABO FALSO
The ruins of the old lighthouse of 1890 and a shipwreck of 1912 lie 5 km/3.1.mi south-west of Cabo San Lucas in the dunes 200 m above sea level. Travel bureaus organise tours, and on the city's beaches you can take a horse for a ride to the Faro Viejo.

SAN JOSÉ DEL CABO MAIN SQUARE
Spruced-up little colonial houses and nostalgic *cobblestone* streets surround the wrought-iron kiosk: in the *Centro Histórico* of the city, a pleasantly relaxed atmosphere prevails; there are good cafés, shops and restaurants – and, of course, *mariachi* bands.

WHALE-WATCHING TOURS
You sail up to within a few metres of the grey whales in small boats, if it's the season. It's only in the winter months that the gentle sea creatures plough through the warm waters of Baja California to go forth and multiply. You can book boat trips almost anywhere for US$35–70/£27.5–56.

WHERE TO GO

`INSIDER TIP` TODOS SANTOS
In this little fishing village (pop. 5,500) just 80 km/50 mi north of Cabo San Lucas ageing rockers, painters and surfers live side by side with the locals. Many who discovered the village by chance simply stayed on. New Age cafés, surfer bars, galleries and restaurants operated by foreigners also attract spoiled New Yorkers. And here it is in real life: the *Hotel California*, which the Eagles once sang about in the song of the same name.

PLAYFUL PRE-COLOMBIANS

As a rule, a pre-Colombian ceremonial centre had a place for a ball game: Totonacs, Mayas, Zapotecs, Aztecs – they all celebrated the ritual game of *pelota*. The court *(tlachtli)* was in the form of a double T; on the lateral boundary walls two stone rings about 50 cm/20 in diameter were fitted. Two teams of three to seven players each had to keep a rubber ball in the air with their shoulders, knees, elbows, body or hips (evidently not with their hands or feet) without the ball touching the ground and shoot it through the ring. The significance and most of the details of the game – for instance, when the game was over – have remained unclear.

TRAVEL TIPS

ADMISSION PRICES

In the larger museums and archaeological sites, expect to be charged 4 to 10 euros; in smaller establishments and private museums, 1 to 5 euros. Only locals and foreigners living in Mexico *(residentes)* have free access to archaeological sites and state-owned museums on Sundays; this does not apply to tourists.

BERTHS

▶ COZUMEL

Cozumel has three berths for cruise ships. From Punta Lagosta you can reach the centre on foot, while the International Pier and the Puerto Maya are about 10 minutes from the city centre by car. Taxis are available.

▶ PROGRESO

With a length of more than 6 km/3,7 mi, the pier at Progreso is seen as one of the world's longest. There is a free shuttle service from the pier to the city centre. Anyone who wants to proceed beyond Mérida will find taxis at the pier as well.

▶ ACAPULCO

In Acapulco cruise ships moor near the centre, near the Zocalo and Fort San Diego. The city centre and the beach can be reached on foot.

▶ MANZANILLO

Manzanillo has cruise ship berths directly at the centre that were opened in 2010. There is another berth in the freight harbour. Taxis and buses are available for getting to the city centre.

▶ PUERTO VALLARTA

The Puerto Vallarta cruise ship terminal is just 5 km/3.1 mi from the city centre, which can be reached by bus or taxi.

▶ CABO SAN LUCAS

Cruise ships must anchor and take their passengers ashore with tenders. From the port, the centre can be reached on foot in about 10 minutes; taxis are available.

EMERGENCY SERVICES

Fire brigade and rescue service: *tel. 060*, police: *tel. 080*
A toll-free emergency service with an information service in English and Spanish is available around the clock everywhere in the country at *tel. 01 80 09 03 92 00.*

HEALTH

There are no inoculation requirements for entering the country. International health insurance with repatriation is definitely recommended. Suntan lotion with a high protection factor and insect repellent should definitely be included in your baggage.

INTERNET & WIFI

In the cities there are still internet cafés that can disappear again as fast as they start up. WiFi is available in restaurants and cafés and now also in many municipalities, often around the Zócalo.

MONEY & CREDIT CARDS

The abbreviation for the peso ($) is the same as that for the US dollar; always

Mexico

Your holiday from start to finish: the main information for your trip

check on the price notices which currency is meant! It is often useful to have dollar notes in lower denominations on hand. Common credit cards are sometimes accepted. The number of ATMs where you can draw cash with a credit card and with an EC card with the Maestro mark (best rate) is increasing.

OPENING HOURS

Businesses are closed in the afternoons (approx. 1pm–4pm) and remain open till late; there are no regulations on closing times. Banks are open Monday through Friday from 9am–4pm, and it is not uncommon for businesses to be open op Sundays.

PHOTOGRAPHY

It's worthwhile buying memory cards in Mexico, as they are cheaper here. In museums you may take photos only against payment. On archaeological sites, there is an extra charge for filming and using a tripod. *Indigenas* do not like being photographed; be sure to get their consent beforehand. In some regions, be cautious whenever you want to take photographs.

TAXI

If a taximeter is fitted, taking a taxi is very economical – 1 km approx. Mex$18 (US$1/£0.61). Otherwise, be sure to negotiate the price beforehand!

TELEPHONE & MOBILE PHONE

There are telephone booths everywhere in the country where you can use telephone cards. One minute to Europe costs 10 pesos, a local call costs 1 peso. European mobile phones can be used in Mexico. A Mexican pre-paid card from Telcel *(www.telcel.com)* costs between 15 and 40 US$ in Mexico – with a call credit for up to half the purchase price. In Europe cards sell for 40–50 euros, but with a credit of only 10 euros. To be able to use it, you need an activated, GSM 1900 compatible device.

TIPPING

In restaurants, 10% to 15% is customary if a *propina* is not already explicitly indicated on the bill. On the other hand, in Mexico taxi drivers do not expect a tip. With 10 pesos, minor favours are normally considered as compensated.

BUDGETING

Coffee	Mex$21–32 (US$1.10–1.70 / £0.90–1.40) *for a café de olla*
Snack	Mex$32–42 (US$1.70–2.20 / £1.35–1.80) *for a taco at a stand*
Beer	Mex$36–53 (US$1.90–2.80 / £1.50–2.20) *for a can*
Souvenir	from Mex$534 (US$28 / £22.50) *for a hammock*
Bus trip	Mex$170–256 (US$9–13.50 / £7.15–10.80) *for 100 km first class*

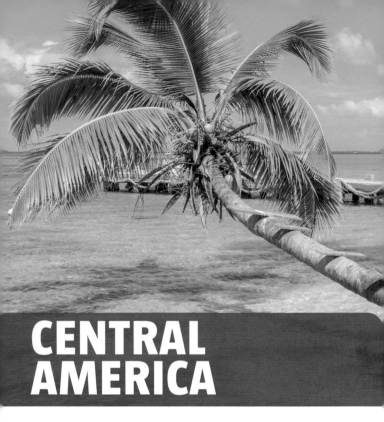

CENTRAL AMERICA

North and South America are joined by a narrow strip of land called Central America. On this relatively small area there are quite a number of small countries, such as Belize, Costa Rica, El Salvador, Honduras and Panama. To the south lies the border with Colombia.

Here you find paradisical landscapes with extensive rainforests, numerous lakes and bizarre volcanoes, picture-perfect white beaches and azure lagoons as well as a large variety of animals to discover. In the nature parks or on boat trips you can observe parrots, raccoons, poison dart frogs, anteaters or howler monkeys. Historically, a separate cultural environment has developed here that has been influenced by the original Indian inhabitants, the European immigrants and African slaves. Accordingly, the cultural highlights are in the first place the fantastic Maya sites, old colonial cities, colourful Indian markets and of course magnificent cities like Panama City with its famous Puente de las Americas, which spans the Panama canal.

BELIZE

(*16/C2*) Belize may be small and rather less well known, but on the other hand it is a country with a huge wow factor. It has the world's second largest reef on its Caribbean coast, where there are also a large number of enchanting islands.

Photo: No wonder that this beach is called Paradise Beach

Seven countries with a common history, but nevertheless individually unique: welcome to Central America

The Cayes, as they are called, are reached by boat, and as from the moment of arrival, the Caribbean lifestyle applies: "no shirt, no shoes, no problem." In the interior the forest areas make out the largest continuous remainder of the tropical rainforest, which can be identified clearly even from space. Unique in the whole world is the jaguar reserve Cockscomb Basin Wildlife Sanctuary, where the mighty large cat still roams free today. And in Anderson's Lagoon you can experience the phenomenon of bioluminescence at night, when schools of fish shine in the water. This palette, already impressive on its own, is supplemented by ancient Maya ruins such as Lamanai, Altun Ha and Xunantunich, one of the greatest jungle metropolises.

BELIZE CITY

(*☐ 16/C2*) **Although all political activity has been moved to Belmopan, the old capital of Belize remains the cultural**

WITNESSES IN THE JUNGLE

As regards archaeological sites, little Belize need not hide behind Mexico, as the country was am important centre of the Maya. *Lamanai* lies on the banks of New River in the lush rainforest, and with a period of occupation of 3000 years it is one of the longest continuously inhabited cities that testify to the Maya culture. In the classical period, up to 20 000 people lived here on 40 000 ha. The most imposing edifices are the nine-tier Jaguar temple and the ball court in which two teams used to compete for dear life to the glory of the gods. If you visit *Altun Ha*, you will come upon an ancient trade centre between the coast and the interior that had many buildings and rich burial gifts in the graves. The most significant find is a jade head weighing 4.5 kg. In *Xunantunich* there are 25 temples and palace buildings around six plazas. Cahal Pech is relatively small, but nevertheless charming and the oldest known Maya city in Belize.

and economic centre of the country. Because of its large port, many different cultures have been assimilated here since the early days, and these give the city its colourful feel today.

The urban scenery is a blend of colourful residential areas, some attractive colonial houses, parks on the sea, busy shopping districts, street markets and many yachts nodding at anchor in the estuary of the Belize River. The river splits Belize into two parts: the mainly commercial South Side and the touristically more attractive North Side.

SIGHTSEEING

BELIZE SWING BRIDGE ★
The bridge is not only the pulsating heart of Belize, but also a rather special construction. It was erected way back in 1897 as a swing bridge and was replaced with a new model from Liverpool in 1923. It is still operated manually today, which makes it unique in the whole world. Its gates are rarely opened now, allowing larger vessels to pass when storms are imminent – then this busy city pauses for a moment.

MARITIME MUSEUM
The museum, which opened in 1996, is located close to the swing bridge in the Maritime Terminal at Haulover Creek. The exhibition tells the story of the region's past and its fishing industry. It is illustrated with numerous model ships and pictures. Probably the most exciting part deals with the Belize Barrier Reef, which was put under the protection of Unesco as a world natural heritage in 1996 because of its abundance of species. It explains the history of its evolution and the associated ecosystem with the multitude of marine animals. *19 Albert St*

MUSEUM OF BELIZE
In 2002, a modern museum was opened in a former prison building in the Fort George Quarter that is dedicated to the country's history. On the ground floor, historical photographs

and documents recall the colonial period and independence as well as the devastating consequences of the hurricane Hattie, which destroyed large parts of Belize in 1961. On the top floor a few Maya treasures are kept, such as pieces of jade, painted ceramics and sculptures. Most of the historical items are scattered across other countries, however. Therefore, the exhibition contains many informative models and explanations of the Maya sites in the country. The museum has also preserved an original cell with the graffiti of the inmates. *Mon–Thu 8.30am–5pm, Fri, Sat 9am–4.30pm | Admission US$10/£7.9 | 5 Eve St, nichbellze.org*

There are elegant jaguars also in Belize's zoo

WHERE TO GO

BELIZE BARRIER REEF ★
The Belize Barrier Reef, which is the world's second largest reef after the Australian Great Barrier Reef, is an absolute highlight. It covers almost 100,000 m²/10 ha and stretches from Belize to the Caribbean Bay islands and on to Honduras. Three of the four atolls that lie here belong to Belize. The Great Blue Hole, a submarine sinkhole (a karst funnel) that is about 125 m deep, is only 80 km/49.7 mi from the capital city of Belize. From the surface, it looks like a large blue hole with a diameter of 330 m/362 yds.

BELIZE ZOO ★
A visit to the zoo in Belize, which includes the Tropical Education Center, is the best way of getting to know the country's animal world. Forty-five different animal species live in the savannah regions. Among the animals, there are the jaguar, jaguarundi and puma, tapirs and ocelots. As for birds, you can see the shy toucan and many more of the 543 species that live in Belize. There are also the amphibians and reptiles, such as frogs, snakes and crocodiles. *Daily 8.30am–5pm | Admission US$15/£11.9 | Mile 29 on the George Price/Western Highway | www. belizezoo.org*

BERTH

▶ BELIZE
Cruise ships anchor off Belize and take their passengers ashore in tenders. For safety reasons, exploring the city on foot is not recommended; it's best to use the taxis, which are available at the cruise terminal, to get around.

GUATEMALA

One thing you cannot say of the country south of the Mexican peninsula of Yucatan is that it's boring. It's not for nothing that this country is also increasingly becoming a tourist destination.

The Maya ruins of Qyiriguá

In Guatemala you will find not only secretive rainforests and volcanoes, black beaches and cloud forests, but also so many relics of the Maya culture that to date it has not been possible to survey them completely. Only in 2018, the use of special laser technology led to the discovery of an enormous, previously unknown Maya settlement in the rainforest in the north of the country – to the great delight of scientists. Hidden under a blanket of vegetation lie an incredible number of at least 60,000 buildings, including a seven-storey pyramid. Such finds from pre-Columbian times testify to the great cultural wealth of the country. After it had been conquered by the Spanish conquistadores in the 16th century, Guatamala remained a Spanish colony until 1921; in 1840, after a period of transition, the country gained independence. Today coffee, banana and sugar exports are the mainstay of the economy of the country, which had been plagued by a civil war that lasted for 36 years.

PUERTO BARRIOS

(📖 16/C3) The port of Puerto Barrios (pop. 60,000) lies on Guatemala's Caribbean coast. Compared with other towns that date back to the colonial period, the city is young, as it only developed around the harbour that was constructed here late in the 19th century. After an earthquake in 1976, a new seaport was built in the immediate vicinity, at Santo Tomás de Castilla, where the cruise ships now moor. From here, you can take trips into the surroundings, as there is hardly anything worth seeing in the city itself.

WHERE TO GO

LAGO DE IZABEL (📖 16/C3)
Not only the Castillo de San Felipe, which was built by the Spaniards in the 17th century, lies on the shore of Guatemala's largest lake. On the other, southern end of the lake, the *Refugio de Vida Silvestre Bocas del Polochic*, which covers more than 200 km^2 /77 mi^2, protects the unique animal life of this humid region, which includes tapirs, howlers and hippopotami. *Approx. 83 km/51.5 mi west of Puerto Barrios*

QUIRIGUÁ

You will probably come across worthwhile Maya sites in Central America more than once during your cruise holiday, but on this site, which has been declared an archaeological park, you can admire an unusually large number of very well preserved sculptures. Those who want to know more about Mayan culture should visit the museum as well. *Approx. 90 km/51.5 mi southwest of Puerto Barrios*

PUERTO QUETZAL

(⌂ 16/B4) **The quetzal is a tropical bird with beautifully colourful plumage – and it is after this bird, the emblem of Guatemala, that the port on the country's western coast (the largest on the Pacific coast) has been named.**

Puerto Quetzal is an industrial city that has little to offer for tourists. Nevertheless, from here you can go on fascinating trips into the country's culture and nature – you will find that during your stay you will be spoilt for choice, whether you would prefer to visit historical Maya sites or would rather visit one of Guatemala's natural wonders.

WHERE TO GO

ANTIGUA GUATEMALA *(⌂ 16/B3)*

Whoever visits this small city (pop. 35,000) in the high country, which from the mid-16th to the mid-18th century was the capital city, will immediately understand why Unesco granted it the status of a World Heritage site. It has a large number of buildings from the colonial period as well as baroque churches. Go admire the convent complex *Convento de las Capuchinas* or *La Merced*, a church from the mid-18th century, behind which rises the imposing volcano *Agua*. That is not the only volcano thereabouts either; the *Acatenango* and the *Volcán de Fuego* are also nearby. *Approx. 82 km/51 mi north of Puerto Quetzal*

LAGO DE ATITLÁN *(⌂ 16/B3)*

What a sight! The water of the country's second largest lake shimmers blue on the highlands, surrounded by three impressive volcanoes. Even the lake itself is of volcanic origin – it lies in the crater of a volcano. The lake, which already impressed the well-travelled nature researcher Alexander Humboldt, may also delight the lover of unique scenery. *Approx. 140 km/51 mi north of Puerto Quetzal*

BERTHS

▶ PUERTO BARRIOS/ SANTO TOMAS DE CASTILLA

Cruise ships moor in an industrial port. As Puerto Barrios has little that is worth seeing, taking a taxi or a water taxi to explore the region is recommended if you don't avail yourself of your cruise operator's excursion packages.

▶ PUERTO QUETZAL

Part of the large industrial port is reserved for incoming cruise ships. Outside the cruise terminal taxis are available, as are local excursion operators. Taxi prices should be negotiated before you get in.

RHYTHMICAL SYMBIOSIS

The dances of the *garifuna*, a people that resulted from the intermarriage of East African slaves with Caribs, are a most colourful spectacle. In the 18th century they had to flee from the Caribbean island of St Vincent and settled on the Atlantic coast of Central America. Today most members of the community live in Honduras, and the largest community has found a home on Roatán. In their dances and music, the two cultures have merged into a rhythmic event that delights the visitors to the island. The performances take place in many island towns, but once a year, on April 12, Punta Gorda takes centre stage when the day of their arrival on Roatán is celebrated with a huge festival.

HONDURAS

This Central American country is gradually being discovered by the tourist industry. Actually, it's odd that this took so long, because Honduras has quite a few things to offer: first-class diving spots on the northern coast, interesting Maya sites in the west and a fantastic, wild nature everywhere.

The almost endless rainforests still cover 30% of the country and reach heights of 1,500 m/4921 ft. The northeastern tip of Honduras is covered by the mosquitia, a humid forest that extends to the Atlantic. The area is characterised by wide forests, rivers and lagoons sheltering a paradisical world of fauna. The greater part of the Pacific coast is highly furrowed and difficult to access, but in return there is the heavenly Caribbean coast, where there are also endless banana, pineapple and citrus plantations. Offshore lie the gorgeous Islas Bahias (Bay Islands), some of which have been developed for tourism. Above all, there is the legendary Maya city of Copán, which has a unique staircase of hieroglyphs with the longest Mayan text found to date.

ROATÁN

(🗺 16/D2) **Off the Honduran coast lie the three Islas de la Bahia, also called the Isles of the Blessed. The largest of the three sisters is Roatán – 8 km/4.97 mi wide, 60 km/37.3 long, with a population of about 30,000, most of whom are employed in the tourism industry.**

Coxen Hole, the island's largest town, is small enough to explore thoroughly on foot. It lies in the south-western part of the island, at the port, where the cruise ships moor. On the other hand, the largest community of Garifunas lives in Punta Gorda, on the other side of the island. That's where you should make a point of watching at least one of their rousing song and dance shows. As yet almost still undiscovered, but nevertheless very attractive and picturesque, is the French Harbour quarter on the southern coast of the island. Some of the houses on the shore are built on piles. You will look for hives of activity in vain on this island; daily life here is peaceful and laid back. Just a few strokes of your flippers off the coast there are coral reefs with small canyons and grottoes that attract enthusiastic divers. In these crystal-clear, pleasantly warm waters you will encounter turtles, rays, moray eels or manta rays. On terra firma there are delightful, white sandy beaches, photogenic mangrove forests and a diverse world of plants and animals. The palms sway in the gentle breeze, and visitors can settle comfortably in the hammocks of the beach bars.

SIGHTSEEING

ARCH'S IGUANA AND MARINE PARK

There's a beautiful tropical garden just outside French Quai where several thousands of iguanas have found a peaceful refuge. Iguanas were a basic element of the island cuisine, but now they are classified as a protected species. The animals are all over the place, so take care while you stroll around: they are likely to just drop from the trees or shrubs unexpectedly. Feeding time is always early in the afternoon. At that time, visitors are allowed to pick the animals up and feed them by hand. *www.archsiguanaand marinepark.com*

BARRIER REEF

If you have already thoroughly explored the home reef of the island, consider the world's second-largest coral reef, which is located quite nearby. The exquisite underwater world of the Belize Barrier Reefs is reached by taking a boat from Roatán. Here the green seagrass sways to the beat of the waves, many-coloured corals and giant cup sponges light up and schools of fish in all colours of the rainbow and of every conceivable shape and size elegantly and resolutely glide through their refuge. With a bit of luck, you may also discover black starfish and the more timid turtles. If you are not too keen on diving, you can still go underwater by taking a mini-submersible at West Bay.

INSIDER TIP DANIEL JOHNSON'S MONKEY AND SLOTH HANGOUT

Have you always wanted to see sloths hanging out in nature? Visit *Daniel Johnson's Monkey & Sloth Hangout* and get up close and personal with these peculiar and lovable animals. This refuge is home not only to sloths, but also houses parrots and monkeys, among others. *Mon–Fri 9am–3pm, Sat 9am–1pm | Admission US$10/£7,9| French Cay monkeyandslothhangout.com*

MAYAN EDEN ECO PARK

The leisure and animal park lies on a height in the jungle above Coxen Hole and can be reached quickly from there. Mayan Eden offers several guided tours every day on which you learn a great

Charming lazybones

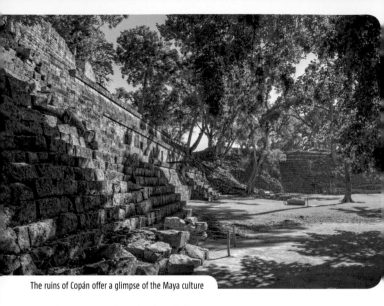

The ruins of Copán offer a glimpse of the Maya culture

deal about nature, the animals and the ancient Maya culture. The route includes a butterfly garden, and you will see hummingbirds dashing about, multicoloured parrots and toucans, various monkey species that will very likely perch on a shoulder and many Maya sculptures, of which the guides will explain the background. For the ultimate adrenalin rush, there is a (properly secured) zipline that takes you from tree to tree in 30 minutes. On the platforms in between you get a marvellous view of the Caribbean sea. *Coxen Hole, facebook.com/MayanEdenEcoPark/*

INSIDER TIP ROATÁN INSTITUTE OF DEEP SEA EXPLORATION

Here an experience of a different order awaits you: with a small submarine, you can dive down as deep as 600 m/1968.5ft, where you will encounter the fascinating underwater world – even in zones of complete darkness. *www. stanleysubmarines.com*

ALEXANDER SHIPWRECK

Divers and adventure junkies have always been fascinated by shipwrecks. Around Roatán there are some of these old relics, which are always shrouded in dramatic stories about pirates. These islands were pirate hideouts for many years; at one time, they offered shelter to more than 10,000 of these corsairs. However, some were sunk only for the divers, who hunt for hidden secrets in the narrow spaces. At the same time, they form a good artificial reef that attracts inhabitants of the seas of all kinds. Within sight of Mahogany Bay, near the cruise ship terminal, you can see one of these half-submerged and rusting ships – a great photographic subject!

FOOD & DRINK

CAFÉ ESCONDIDO

Healthy dining with a view. The café in the West End offers not only a great view of the port, but also breakfasts, dishes inspired by Asian cuisine, salads and fresh smoothies. *Mon, Thu–Sun 7.45am–4pm | West End Road*

ROATAN OASIS

The menu changes every two weeks, only fresh ingredients are used and people with every possible preference, from fish to meat to vegetarians and vegans find something that delights their palate here. *Mon–Fri 5pm–8.30pm| Carretera Principal, West End | Tel. +504 94 846 659 | www.roatanoasis.com*

PUERTO CORTÉS

(🕮 16/C3) **The city was founded on the northern coast of Honduras by the Spanish conquistadores in 1524.**

As the corsairs were committing their deeds most foul in the Caribbean up into the 18th century and the unfortified town was attacked by them time and again, Puerto Cortés remained rather thinly populated. The town only became economically active in the 20th century on the back of banana exports and when a railway line was laid. Today Puerto Cortés has the largest seaport in Honduras. For travellers, there is nothing worth seeing in the city itself; it serves primarily as a point of departure for trips into the interior.

WHERE TO GO

COPÁN *(🕮 16/C3)*

There is a significant archaeological site of the Mayan civilisation at Copán, approx. 235 km/146 mi south-west of Puerto Cortés. In the *Parque Arqueológico y Sepulturas (daily 8am–4pm | admission US$15 US/£11.9)* you dig into the history of the fascinating lost culture of the early inhabitants of Central America; temples, altars and stone stelea testify to the high level of development reached by the Maya, who were already living here more than 1000 years BC. In the excellent *Museo de Escultura (daily 8am –4pm | Admission US$7/£5.5)* a large number of sculptures from the Maya period are on show.

OMOA

(🕮 16/C3) About 13 km west of Puerto Cortés lies the little harbour town of Omoa, the outstanding feature of which is its beach, which is located in a wide bay. The *Fortaleza de San Fernando Omoa*, a fort to ward off pirate attacks, dates back to the middle of the 18th century. The monumental complex covers an area of approximately 4400 m^2/0.44 ha, which makes it the largest in Central America. *Mon–Fri 9am–5pm, Sat, Sun 9am–4pm | Admission US$4/£3.15*

BERTHS

▶ PUERTO CORTÉS

In Puerto Cortés the cruise ships moor in the industrial harbour. Since the safety situation is sometimes not optimal, it's better to book a place on the organised tours of the shipping line in question.

▶ ROATÁN/COXEN HOLE

On Roatán cruise ships moor either directly in Coxen Hole, within walking distance to the centre, or at the Mahogany Bay Cruise Center, which is about 7 km/4,4 mi east of Coxen Hole. Taxis and rental cars are available for exploring the island.

EL SALVADOR

(📖 16/B–C4) **Just about 300 km²
smaller than Wales, El Salvador has a
very diverse landscape on a small area.**
In this smallest country of Central America, volcanoes soaring more than 2000 m/
6560 ft are as much part of the landscape as long beaches with dark sand
on the Pacific coast, forests and coffee
plantations and, in the cities, an architecture influenced by the colonial style. And
as elsewhere in the region, in El Salvador
you also come across the pre-Columbian
products of the Maya, who populated
the country before the Spaniards conquered it in 1525. El Salvador gained
independence in the mid-19th century.

ACAJUTLA

(📖 16/B4) **Acajutla is the most important port on El Salvador's Pacific coast
and gained economic importance only
under Spanish rule.**
This is where cruise ships passing the
western coast of Central America moor,
and it is also from here that coffee, sugar and textiles are exported all over the
world. Acajutla is the ideal starting point
for exploring some of the beauties of this
country, which to date has been underestimated as a tourist destination.

BERTH

▶ **EL SALVADOR**
In Acajutla cruise ships moor in the
industrial port. For those who want
to explore the area on their own,
there are taxis near the port.

WHERE TO GO

INSIDER TIP ▶ **EL CARMEN ESTATE**
(📖 16/B4)
If you want to become acquainted with
one of the country's most important
products and its manufacture, your visit
to this plantation, which has a hotel
as well as a restaurant, will not have
been in vain. On guided tours, you will
learn about coffee production, and of
course you can do some coffee tasting
as well. If you want something more
adventurous, you can fly across the
plantation on a zipline. *Guided tours
US$5/22.50/£3.9/17.8 | km 97 carretera
Ahuachapan-Sonsonate, Concepción de
Ataco | www.elcarmenestate.com | approx. 53 km/33 mi north of Acajutla*

PARQUE NACIONAL LOS VOLCANOS
(CERRO VERDE NATIONAL PARK)
(📖 16/B4)
Encompassing the volcanoes *Cerro Verde*,
Izalco and *Santa Ana*, this national park
reaches an altitude of more than 2000
m/6560 ft. You can admire the volcanoes from various ☼ viewing points.
Also of volcanic origin is the perfectly
beautiful *Lago de Coatepeque*, which
was formed in a volcanic crater and resembles a blue eye gazing into the sky.
*Approximately 80 km/50 mi north-east
of Acajutla*

TAZUMAL & JOYA DE CERÉN
(📖 16/B4 & 16/C4)
The ruins of the significant Maya settlement of Tazumal lie in the city of Chalchuapa. There are two temple pyramids
on the site. A truly unique archaeological
treasure is ★ *Joya de Cerén*, which after an eruption of the volcano Ilopango
remained very well preserved under the
ash and gives us a picture of the daily
life of the simple farmers of the Maya

period. *Tazumal approx. 75 km/46.6 mi north, Joya de Cerén approx. 73 km/ 45.3 km north-east of Acajutla*

NICARAGUA

The country lies between the Caribbean in the east and the Pacific in the west; along the Pacific coast it is defined by a range of volcanoes, but in addition there are rainforests, fantastic beaches, the enormous Lake Nicaragua (the largest lake of Central America), and a friendly population.

Formerly plagued by civil wars, the country is now increasingly becoming known as a destination for travellers – not only because of its natural attractions, but also because it is pervaded by an original charm that has remained largely unaffected by the Western lifestyle.

SAN JUAN DEL SUR

(*17/B2*) **San Juan del Sur (pop. approx. 7800) lies in the west of Nicaragua, on the Pacific coast, and is increasingly visited by cruise ships of operators who want to show their passengers the beauty of the country.**

Little more than a fishing village, San Juan del Sur has some beaches worth visiting, a beach promenade with numerous restaurants that have mostly seafood on the menu, and a market with products of the country.

SIGHTSEEING

CRISTO DE LA MISERICORDIA ☀
The monumental statue of Christ was erected above San Juan del Sur in 2009. From up here you have a spectacular, panoramic view of the horseshoe-shaped bay and the town.

WHERE TO GO

GRANADA (*17/B1*)
Below the Mombacho volcano lies the city, which was established by the Spaniards in the early 16th century and still impresses visitors with its colonial buildings and its huge cathedral. Granada lies in front of the breathtaking backdrop of *Lake Nicaragua*, which you can also explore from here. To the south of the city lies the *Reserva Natural Volcán Mombacho*; here you can take a short circular path around the crater through the cloud forest and familiarise yourself with the multifaceted nature (*www.mombacho.org*). *Approx. 98 km/ 60.9 mi north of San Juan del Sur*

PARQUE NACIONAL VOLCÁN MASAYA (*17/A1*)
The two volcanoes Masaya and Nindirí in the national park are still active; after 2016 a new lava lake appeared in the Santiago crater – a spectacular, fiery sight. *Approx. 105 km/60.9 mi north of San Juan del Sur*

BERTH

▶ **NICARAGUA**
Cruise ships anchor in port and take their passengers ashore in tenders. The cruise ship operators offer trips into the area, but you also have option to explore the region with the aid of local operators, e.g. *Nicaragua Tour Network (www.nicaraguatournetwork. com) or to use a taxi.*

The green basilisk: a specimen of Costa Rica's exotic wildlife

COSTA RICA

Bubbling volcanoes that light up the night sky with a pyrotechnic display of glowing red magma, butterflies the size of your palm and tiny hummingbirds that suck the nectar from the jungle flowers – more than 30 regions have been designated protected areas.

Probably unique in the world: over one quarter of the surface area of this country is protected – as national parks and biosphere reserves, but also as Indian reservations and areas that Unesco has declared World Heritage Sites. Steaming rainforests, mist-shrouded high valleys, ochre-hued savannahs, mangrove swamps and dry forests, mountain chains and volcanoes, meandering rivers, coral reefs and green islands off the coast: they are all part of the country's extraordinary beauty and worthy of protection.

PUERTO LIMÓN

(🗺 17/C2) **Puerto Limón (pop. 80,000) is one of the country's main harbours, a container port for coffee, pineapples and bananas and the centre of Afro-Caribbean culture.**

The city has suffered from earthquakes, and evidence of the destruction can still be seen in the cityscape today. The land on which the Parque Vargas *(daily | Admission free | 1st St/2nd Avenue)* is laid out, near the harbour, was donated to the city by a fruit-growing company. Created at the end of the 19th century, it offers an insight into the vegetation of the Caribbean. From the pavilion you have a 🌿 marvellous view of the sea.

SIGHTSEEING

CORREO

The large corner house, built at the turn of the century before last, has the loveliest windows, balconies and doors in town, and is painted in pretty pastel shades. *South side of the Mercado Municipal*

MUSEO ETHNOHISTÓRICO

The exhibits in the ethnological museum illustrate the pre-Columbian population and the arrival of Columbus. Illustrated panels provide information on the history of the region. Impressive: the exhibition of the construction of the railway to Limón. *Tue–Sat 9am–noon and 1pm–4pm | US$1/£0.8 | Av. 2/C/ 4 | South side of the Mercado in the old post office | 2/C/ 4 |First floor*

WHERE TO GO

BRIBÍ (*ll 17/C2*)

The town is home to Talamanca Indians, who work hard at harvest time for little remuneration, and a destination for travellers who are interested in the culture of the *indígenas*. The village, with its basic wooden houses surrounded by banana plantations, lies 60 km/37.3 mi south of Puerto Limón on the border with Panama, and together with its surrounding area it makes up an Indian reservation. The meeting place is the turquoise *Restaurante Bribrí (tel. 27 51 00 44 | Budget)*.

CAHUITA (*ll 17/C2*)

A palm-fringed road, beach to the left, banana plantations to the right, plus red achiote trees (whose fruits the pre-Columbian population used as a dye) runs 43 km/26.7 mi south from Limón to the village of Cahuita, the meeting place for young people who lead a relaxed life on the beach and appreciate the exotically flavoured food in the sodas and the cheap beds in the small hotels. Music and conviviality are the order of the day. The centre of the town with the north entrance to the national park has basic hotels, cabinas and restaurants, but

is less attractive; moreover, you have to keep an eye on your belongings.

The *Cahuita National Park (daily 8am–5pm | Donations appreciated)* – one of the loveliest national parks in Costa Rica, with swamp and mangrove forest, toucans, hummingbirds and ara parrots, monkeys, raccoons and sloths, as well as wonderful white beaches – reaches from Cahuita across the north-eastern peninsula at Puerto Vargas and south along the beach to Punta Caliente. The well-maintained main trail leads through the forest, parallel to the coast and beach. Admission to the national park is free from Kelly Creek. An offshore coral reef is home to almost three dozen types of coral and over 100 different tropical fish.

PUERTO VIEJO DE TALAMANCA (*ll 17/C2*)

The good vibes are in the air: this colourful, lively resort with numerous hotels, restaurants and bars, plus a dark beach, 15 km/9.3 mi south of Cahuita, is a meeting place for young travellers. The hot days are spent playing beach volleyball, and there's surfing between December and April. Don't forget your insect repellent, and watch out for the current in the sea! The ⓥ **INSIDER TIP** *Asociación Talamanqueña de Ecoturismo y Conservación (C/ Principal | PuertoViejodeTalamanca |tel.2750 0191|www.ateccr.org)*, an organisation for ecotourism and nature conservation, offers fabulous trekking and river tours to the indigenous peoples in the jungle of the Atlantic region. Well worth a visit – especially with children – is the ⓥ **INSIDER TIP** *Centro de Rescate Jaguar (www.jaguarrescue.foundation)* in Playa Chiquita, a rescue centre for orphaned and injured wild animals, which are lovingly looked after and pampered here.

PUNTARENAS

(🏛 17/B2) **Puntarenas, which expanded with the coffee trade, covers a 6-km/3.7-mi headland in the Gulf of Nicoya and seals off the lagoon and El Estero Bay in the south.**

The humid, subtropical climate is ideal for growing the rice, bananas and coconut palms for which Puntarenas is still a trading centre. On the southern side of the city there is a long stretch of beach where the locals have their second homes – this is where the boats are.

SIGHTSEEING

Because of the heat and humidity, it's best to stroll on the peninsula – which is about 50 Calles long and only four or five Avenidas wide – in the morning or after 4pm.

BERTHS

▶ PUERTO LIMÓN
You can reach the city centre on foot from the cargo harbour, where the cruise ships moor. Taxis are available in the harbour; you can negotiate prices with the drivers.

▶ PUNTARENAS
In Puntarenas there are two berths for cruise ships. One is near the city centre; the other is in the industrial port of Puerto Caldera and is about a 20-minute drive from the city centre. In this port taxis are available if you want to drive farther.

A stroll along the beach promenade *Paseo de los Turistas* (southern side) will take you past pleasant restaurants, cafés and bars; to the north of the city, you'll pass the harbour basin with wharfs, warehouses and ferry terminals – the working world of a port. The downtown streets *(Calles 1–7)* and the market *(Mercado Municipal) (Av. 3/C/ 2)* are abuzz with action.

MUSEO HISTÓRICO DE LA CIUDAD DE PUNTARENAS
There are little exhibitions telling the history of the city, its port and coffee exports. The black-and-white pictures taken at the turn of the 19th century are interesting. *Mon–Fri 9am–noon, 1pm–5pm | Admission free| Av. Central/C/ 1 | Casa de la Cultura*

PARQUE MARINO DEL PACÍFICO
The attractions include the crocodile breeding basins, the turtles, the injured pelicans found and cared for here and the tropical fish in the beautifully designed state park, which is committed to protecting the ocean. *Tue–Sun 9am–4.30pm | US$10.£7.9 | Av. 4 | Old station, 500 m/545 yds east of the mole for cruise ships | www.parquemarino.org*

PLAZA CENTRAL
The role of the Parque Central is assumed here by a small plaza with a 100-year-old, massive sandstone church. A pedestrian zone starts at the north-eastern end of the square *(C/5–7)*.

SHOPPING

The Mercado Central not only offers groceries, but also crafts and souvenirs. *Av. 3/C/ 32*

PANAMA

More than just the Panama Canal: the country offers landscape features, exotic fauna and architectural extremes.

In two senses, it is a picture-book country: Janosch's tiger duck never did reach Panama, but the children's book sings the praises of the beautiful, exotic country – and that actually really exists. The Central American country is no longer an official part of the Caribbean, but there are plenty of heavenly beaches for sunbathing and surfing here as well – after all, Panama has a coastline of almost 2000 km/1250 mi. At the narrowest point of this elongated country, the Pacific and the Atlantic coast are just 80 km/49.7 mi apart. The famous Panama Canal, which was opened in 1914, was dug across this isthmus and allows ships to reach their destination faster, more cheaply and with less risk, as they need not sail around Cape Horn at the tip of South America. West and east of this canal you can satisfy your hunger for adventure to the max in the country's natural paradises. Dense jungles, verdant mountains, valleys or roaring rivers – it's all there in the smallest possible space.

BOCAS DEL TORO

(🛇 17/D3) **Bocas del Toro (mouths of the bull), capital of the eponymous province near the border with Costa Rica, lies on the southernmost end of the Isla Colón – not to be confused with the city of Colón, more than 600 km/373 mi further to the west.** The Isla Colón is part of an archipelago with six large and numerous smaller islands, which with its dream beaches and tropical nature is emblematic of the Caribbean. The city of Bocas del Toro, founded as recently as the early 20th century by the United Fruit Company, brims with Caribbean charm, with its colourful little wooden houses and the relaxed lifestyle of its residents.

There's much to explore in the sea at Bocas del Toro

Shortens the voyage: The Panama Canal links the Atlantic with the Pacific

SIGHTSEEING

FINCA LOS MONOS

In this magical, private botanical garden just outside the city centre, you can experience the riot of colour of the exotic plants; howling monkeys swing through the trees; sloths leisurely clamber along branches (when they get around to it), and butterflies in all imaginable colours flutter around flowers rich in nectar. *Guided tours of the garden Mon 1pm and Fri 8.30am | Admission US$10/£7.9 | www.bocasdeltorobotanicalgarden.com*

WHERE TO GO

BASTIMENTOS NATIONAL PARK
(*17/D3*)

This national park includes the Isla Bastimentos (an island east of the Isla Colón), numerous small islands and the sea, and has an area exceeding 13000 ha. It includes valuable coral reefs, lush mangroves, tortoises and sloths and a colourful underwater world that can be explored by snorkelling, for example. *Can be reached by water taxi from Bocas del Torro*

COLÓN

(*18/A1*) **This important port in the north of Panamas is also the point of arrival for cruise ships sailing in the Caribbean.**

Colón flourished at the time the Panama Canal, which links the Pacific to the Atlantic, was under construction. Although Colón has the world's second largest free trade zone, where you can shop duty free near the port, there is little to see in the city area; furthermore, as it is not regarded as very safe, going about on foot is not recommended.

WHERE TO GO

GATÚN LAKE (*18/A2*)

One consequence of the construction of the Panama Canal is the huge artificial Gatún Lake, through which the shipping lane follows a specially marked gully. For smaller ships and pleasure craft, there is an alternative route. As a dam, it supplies water to the country's population and industry and covers the water needs of the locks as well. It has also become a popular travel destination, as the plant and animal world of these parts is very interesting. When the formerly densely vegetated valley was flooded, the tops of some of the hills remained above water and became islands. On the largest of these, the *Barro Colorado* Island, a highly regarded scientific institution was established where researchers of the tropics from all over the world carry out their studies.

PANAMA CITY (*18/A–B2*)

The country's capital is a city of extremes. Not only because of its size and number of inhabitants (about half of the 3.3 million inhabitants of the country live here), but also for architectural reasons. The contrast between the ultramodern western part of the city and the Casco Antiguo, the historical part (which is a Unesco World Cultural Heritage site) could not be greater. This quarter, which dates back to 1673, should definitely be explored on foot. It bears the stamp of Spanish and French colonial edifices, painted in bright colours and with elaborately decorated wrought iron balconies planted with many flowers. This is also where all worthwhile sights are found. There's a great view of the skyline and the Panama Canal from the colourful *Biomuseo (Edificio 136, Calzada de Amador)*, designed by Frank Gehry.

PANAMA CANAL ★ (*18/A2*)

From the port of Colón you can take a boat to explore the world-famous Panama Canal. Not only is it a technical masterpiece, but it is also very much worth seeing from an environmental point of view. Here the dense forest reaches down to the water's edge, which enables travellers on the water to observe the luxuriant vegetation as well as many exotic animals. Howlers, crocodiles, tortoises, lizards and a marvellous bird world have found an almost undisturbed refuge in this area, to which access was limited until recently. Along the canal there is a railway line that runs from Colón to Panama City. Initially, this line was used only for freight transport, but since 2001 it is also used for a luxury passenger train with panoramic windows. For the train, it's a one-hour trip; the large ships need nine hours to complete the waterway.

BERTHS

▶ **BOCAS DEL TORO**

In Bocas del Toro, cruise ships cannot moor in the port, they have to anchor outside. Passengers are taken ashore in tenders.

▶ **COLÓN**

Colón has two piers for cruise ships: the older Cristobal Pier, which is not used very often, and the modern Colón 2000 Cruise Terminal. For excursions organised by the shipping lines, there are vehicles on standby near the berth. For travellers who want to go off on their own, there are taxis available outside the port. You negotiate the price before taking off.

TRAVEL TIPS

BELIZE

MONEY & CURRENCY
In Belize the Belize dollar (BZD) is the common means of payment, but the US$ and major credit cards are frequently accepted as well. These can also be used to draw money at ATMs.

HEALTH
As a rule, doctors and hospitals must be paid directly.

LANGUAGE
The official language is English.

TELEPHONE & INTERNET
In Belize a GSM 1900 network is used. In Belize city, free WiFi is available in some restaurants and shops.

COSTA RICA

MONEY & CURRENCY
Costa Rica's currency is the Colón. Prices are indicated in US$. Even in smaller towns there are ATMs that accept international bank cards. Banks are open Mon–Fri 9am–3pm. Credit cards (Visa, Amex) are widely accepted.

HEALTH
Medical care in the capital city is excellent. A risk of malaria and dengue fever exists in the coastal regions and in areas below 600 m.
Protect yourself with suitable clothing and insect repellents.

LANGUAGE
The official language is Spanish.

TELEPHONE & INTERNET
WiFi is not widely distributed in Costa Rica yet. You will find a list of internet cafés at *www.cybercafes.com*, and of WiFi hotspots at *www.hotspotlocations.com*. Public telephones are everywhere; they are used with telephone cards with a chip code or a PIN code. You can also use prepaid cards of local service providers for your telephone.

EL SALVADOR

MONEY & CURRENCY
In El Salvador payments are made in US$. The usual credit cards are accepted in shops and restaurants. You can draw cash at ATMs

HEALTH
Outside San Salvador, medical care is inadequate and not at a modern level.

LANGUAGE
The official language of El Salvador is Spanish.

TELEPHONE & INTERNET
The mobile phone networks in El Salvador use the GSM standards 850, 900 and 1950. Internet cafés can be found especially in areas frequented by tourists; free WiFi is readily available only in the capital of San Salvador.

GUATEMALA

MONEY & CURRENCY
In Guatemala the coin of the realm is the (Q); US$ is accepted by some dealers. You can use your EC card or credit card at some ATMs to draw money.

HEALTH
Healthcare does not come up to European standards.

Central America

**Your holiday from start to finish:
the main information for your trip**

LANGUAGE
The national language in Guatemala is Spanish.

TELEPHONE & INTERNET
There are internet cafés in Guatemala. Free WiFi is frequently available in cities and tourist centres.

HONDURAS

MONEY & CURRENCY
The national currency in Honduras is the lempira (HNL). It is also often possible to pay with US$. Major credit cards are accepted. Credit cards can also be used to draw money from ATMs.

HEALTH
Outside large cities, medical care is inadequate; hospitals ask for an advance payment.

LANGUAGE
The official language in Honduras is Spanish.

TELEPHONE & INTERNET
The major mobile service providers have concluded the necessary roaming contracts with Honduras. You will find internet cafés in the larger cities, and free WiFi is available in cities on squares, in parks and in some restaurants.

NICARAGUA

MONEY & CURRENCY
The official currency of the country is the Córdoba (NIO), but US$ are also accepted. You can draw cash at ATMs with a major credit card or with the EC card. Shops and restaurants often accept credit cards.

HEALTH
Treatments and medicines must be paid immediately at the point of service. Medical care is often inadequate and does not come up to European standards.

LANGUAGE
The national language is Spanish; in addition, English is also spoken to a limited extent in some places.

TELEPHONE & INTERNET
It is advisable to buy an economical prepaid card locally. Free WiFi is available in many places in the capital city of Managua, and in San Juan del Sur some cafés also offer free WiFi.

PANAMA

MONEY & CURRENCY
The official currency is the Balboa. It is linked 1:1 to the US dollar. The US$ is also accepted as a means of payment. In larger cities, major credit cards are frequently accepted. You can use an EC card to draw cash at ATMs.

HEALTH
Treatments and medicines must in most cases be paid immediately at the point of service. Medical care in Panama frequently does not come up to European standards.

LANGUAGE
Panama's official language is Spanish.

TELEPHONE & INTERNET
It is often cheaper to buy a prepaid card on site. Free WiFi is often available in larger cities and often in restaurants as well.

COLOMBIA

Colombia has only recently become one of the trendy South American countries. There is a new spirit of optimism in this Andean country after peace efforts have borne fruit and tourists can now return and rediscover the multifaceted local nature and culture.

Owing to its position on the equator, the landscape presents many different faces: cloud forests, desert regions, the mountain range of the Andes with its volcanoes and glaciers, but the Pacific and Atlantic beaches as well. If it gets a little too hot for you on the undeveloped Caribbean shores, take a trip of less than half an hour by car into the mountains and you will feel distinctly refreshed in the lush vegetation. Thus lovers of the most diverse scenery get their money's worth in this country. And let's not forget the coffee lovers: the expansive coffee plantations on the green highlands produce an excellent Arabica coffee.

CARTAGENA

(🏛 18/D1) **This old colonial city on the sea is described as the most beautiful metropolis in all of Columbia. Cartagena was founded by Spanish conquistadores in 1533 and quickly grew into an important port for trading vessels.**

In the cobblestone streets of the Old Town, the ambience is one of lively and colourful hustle and bustle, and the flair is fascinating. Here you will find flawlessly restored palaces, residential houses

Breathtaking nature meets eventful history: Colombia is a South American pearl waiting to be discovered

with balconies and romantic courtyards, imposing churches and monasteries, restaurants and street cafés – and it's all decorated with exuberant displays of beautiful flowers. The historical city centre is completely walled in and is part of the Unesco World Heritage. It's a lovely place for dawdling about after dusk, when there are buskers playing in the squares, delectable street food is sold on the sidewalks and many restaurants have put their tables and chairs out in the streets where no traffic is allowed.

FORTALEZA SAN FELIPE ★

Cartagena's Old Town itself may already a fortress, but the Spaniards erected fortifications outside the city walls as well, for example the mighty *Castillo de San Felipe de Barajas*. It is the strongest stronghold the Spaniards ever built in their colonies, and in fact it was never taken. Construction started in the mid-17th century, and part of the strategy was a complex tunnel

THROUGH SICKNESS TO FAME

In 2016, the winner of the Nobel prize for literature, Gabriel García Márquez, who had died two years earlier, found his last place of rest in Cartagena, the city that had played such a great role in his work. For example, it was the setting of his epic novel "Love in the time of Cholera". His urn was put in the courtyard of the former monastery La Merced, where a bust of him is also located. About 500 m farther you pass the Casa García Márquez, which you will recognise by his portrait on the façade. Although Márquez lived in Mexico because of the unrest in his home country, he kept returning to Cartagena, which he described as his favourite town. The house is not open to the public, however.

system that passed on even the slightest sounds made by intruders. On a guided tour of the complex, you can learn more about the cunning inventions of the military technician Antonio de Aréval.

MONASTERY LA POPA

The highest point of the city is crowned by the *Convento de la Popa*, an edifice that looks like a castle but was originally built as an Augustinian convent in 1606. Because of its position, it gives you a splendid view of the whole city. But the inner courtyard, adorned with flowers, and the museum there are very well worth visiting too. In the chapel you can admire a statue of Cartagena's patron saint, Señora de la Candelaria. Her feast day is celebrated on February 2 with a huge pilgrimage. Visitors who are not accustomed to the heat should not attempt the strenuous ascent on foot. Taxis take the hairpin bends of this road faster and more safely. *Tue–Sun 8.30am–5.30pm | Calle 37*

MUSEO DEL ORO ZENÚ

To be sure, the gold museum in the capital city of Bogotá is the largest of its kind. But even its little sister in Cartagena makes it quite clear how valuable and fascinating the ornaments and other exhibits from the pre-Colombian period are, which for

the greater part were crafted from gold. Their creators, the Zenú, lived in this region before it was colonised by the Spaniards and left delicately worked ornaments, coins and display pieces behind. It is also a nice little place because of the comfortable air conditioning. *www.banrepcultural.org/ cartagena/ museo-del-oro-zenu-1*

MUSEO NAVAL DEL CARIBE

In an impressive building formerly used as a Jesuit college and hospital, a museum dedicated to shipping was opened in 1992 to celebrate the 500th anniversary of the discovery of America by Columbus. There are model ships from many earlier centuries and glass cabinets with maquettes depicting scenes from the naval battles that were fought around Cartagena. Furthermore, you can discover historical maps and a variety of weapons that originally belonged to pirates. Sometimes guided tours are offered in English. *Daily 9am–5pm | Calle San Juán de Dios No. 3–62 | www.museonavaldelcaribe.com*

PALACIO DE LA INQUISICIÓN

Opposite the gold museum, facing the Plaza Bolivar, a fine historical building from the 18th century houses an exhibition on the city's history. In several parts of the building, the inquisition of the Spanish colonial masters, the construction of the railway from Cartagena to Calanar, the commercial port, slavery and influences of African culture as

Colonial architecture is found in the Old Town every step of the way

The saleslady's dress is as colourful as the fruit she is selling

well as the colonial building style are represented. Unfortunately, many of the display boards are only in Spanish; only a few are in English. But even then, the instruments of torture are scary enough.

SHOPPING

Right inside the 15 m thick city wall, *Las Bóvedas* is an interesting place to shop for handicrafts and souvenirs. Cells subsequently used as storerooms have been transformed into 23 shops. Products typical of the city and the region are hammocks, handbags and travel bags, embroidered men's shirts, woollen blankets and, of course, coffee. On the streets fruit vendors tout their deep red watermelons, cut mangoes or papayas with salt on their wooden pushcarts. The very courageous can also venture into the labyrinthine *Mercado de Bazurto,* which is an experience for all your senses. If you are in the know, you can acquire gems at reasonable prices here. Colombian emeralds are among the world's best. For that purpose, the Castillo Grande is the best place to go.

TASTY FAST FOODS

In Colombia, the typical *comida corriente* (translated: fast food) is a piece of meat with some vegetables. From the Paisa region, with its huge herds of cattle, comes the bandeja paisa, a typical dish of the region, which is, of course, appropriately substantial, as befits the countryside. It contains much meat, such as steak, mince, a sausage or fried pork belly, which comes with plantain, fried egg, avocado, kidney beans and rice. If that is not enough, you can add *artepas* on the side – round maize pancakes, which you can also have with a variety of fillings. Other favourites are *ceviche* (a marinated raw fish) and *empanadas* (rolled maize pancakes with beans, cheese, meat and potatoes), *buñuelos,* (fried dough balls) or *tamales* (pancakes steamed in maize leaves and filled with meat and paprika).

TRAVEL TIPS

 Colombia: the most important information for your trip

BERTH

In Cartagena cruise ships moor in the industrial port, which is about 4 km/2.5 mi from the centre of the city. For cruise ships there are a total of six berths available. You can take a free shuttle bus to the cruise ship terminal; there are taxis in as well as outside the port, with the taxis outside the port being the more economical as a rule.

HEALTH

No inoculations are compulsory for entering Colombia. In larger cities you can expect medical care similar to that in Europe, but the rural regions are a different matter. For that reason, it is advisable to see to it that you have suitable international medical cover with repatriation. Taking along a small emergency kit is always a good idea; in any case, insect repellent and sunscreen lotion as well as medication for diarrhoea should be part of it.

LANGUAGE

The official language in Colombia is Spanish.

MONEY & CURRENCY

The coin of the realm is the Columbian peso (COP). Both the euro and the peso can be changed for dollars without any problems. You can generally also draw cash at ATMs with the major credit cards, e.g. Visa or Mastercard, as well as with the EC card.

TELEPHONE & INTERNET

If you want to use a Columbian prepaid card, you must have an activated mobile phone. In Cartagena there are numerous free WiFi hotspots, especially in cafés and restaurants.

TIPPING

In restaurants a tip of around 10% of the account is expected. In some restaurants this 10% is already included under the heading *servicio*. However, if you were not satisfied, you need not pay this amount. Taxi drivers do not expect a tip.

BUDGETING

Meal	approx. US$10 / £8 *for a 3-course menu in a mid-range restaurant*
Beer	approx. US$1 / £0.80 *for 0.5 l*
Water	approx. US$0.56 / £0.45 *for 0.33 l*
Taxi	US$1.70 / £1.36 *per kilometre*

USEFUL PHRASES

ENGLISH	SPANISH

IN BRIEF

ENGLISH	SPANISH
yes/no/maybe	sí/no/quizás
please/thank you	por favor/gracias
Sorry!	¡Perdona!
Excuse me!	¡Perdone!
May I ...?	¿Puedo ...?
Pardon?	¿Cómo dice?
I would like to ...	Querría ...
Have you got ...?	¿Tiene usted ...?
How much is ...?	¿Cuánto cuesta ...?
I (don't) like this.	Esto (no) me gusta.
good/bad	bien/mal
open/closed	abierto/cerrado

SALUTATION & TRAVEL

ENGLISH	SPANISH
Good morning!/afternoon!	¡Buenos días!/días!
Good evening!/night!	¡Buenas tardes!/noches!
Hello!/Goodbye!/Bye!	¡Hola!/¡Adiós!/¡Hasta luego!
My name is ...	Me llamo ...
What's your name?	¿Cómo se llama usted?
I'm from ...	Soy de ...
station/harbour	estación/puerto
departure/arrival	salida/salida/llegada
What time is it?	¿Qué hora es?
It's three o'clock.	Son las tres.
today/tomorrow/yesterday	hoy/mañana/ayer

FOOD & DRINK

ENGLISH	SPANISH
The menue, please.	¡El menú, por favor!
May I have ...?	¿Podría traerme ... por favor?
knife/fork/spoon	cuchillo/tenedor/cuchara
salt/pepper/sugar	sal/pimienta/azúcar
vinegar/oil	vinagre/aceite
milk/cream/lemon	leche/crema/limón
with/without ice	con/sin hielo
vegetarian	vegetariano
May I have the bill, please?	Querría pagar, por favor.

Short and sweet

This short list of phrases will help you say the most important words and phrases in the languages listed below:

FRENCH	DUTCH
oui/non/peut-être	ja/nee/misschien
s'il vous plaît/merci	alsjeblieft/bedankt
Pardon!	Pardon!
Pardon!	Neem me niet kwalijk!
Puis-je ...?	Mag ik ...?
Comment?	Pardon?
Je voudrais ...	Ik wil graag ...
Avez-vous ...?	Heeft u ...?
Combien coûte ...?	Hoeveel kost ...?
Ça (ne) me plaît (pas).	Dat vind ik (niet) leuk.
bon/mauvais	goed/slecht
ouvert/fermé	open/gesloten
Bonjour!/	Goeden morgen/
Bonjour!	dag!
Bonsoir!/Bonne nuit!	Goeden avond!/nacht!
Salut!/Au revoir!/	Hallo!/Dag!
Salut!	Doei!
Je m'appelle ...	Ik heet ...
Quel est votre nom?	Hoe heet u?
Je suis de ...	Ik kom uit ...
gare/port	station/haven
départ/départ/arrivée	vertrektijd/aankomst
Quelle heure est-il?	Hoe laat is het?
Il est trois heures	Het is drie uur
aujourd'hui/demain/	vandaag/morgen/
hier	gisteren
La carte, s'il vous plaît.	De kaart, alstublieft.
Puis-je avoir ...	Mag ik ...?
s'il vous plaît	
couteau/fourchette/	mes/fork/
cuillère	lepel
sel/poivre/sucre	zout/peper/suiker
vinaigre/huile	azijn/olie
lait/crème/citron	melk/room/citroen
avec/sans glaçons	met/zonder ijs
végétarien(ne)	vegetariër
Je voudrais payer,	Mag ik afrekenen.
s'il vous plaît.	

HOW TO CRUISE

EMBARKING

On arrival at the cruise terminal, you hand over your baggage. Remember to put important items you will need after you have gone aboard in your hand luggage, as it may take quite a while before the suitcases are brought to the relevant cabins. At the check-in point you will get your boarding pass and a security check. If you are lucky, you can go on board immediately, but it is also possible that you may have to stay in the waiting hall a little longer before it's your turn.

DISEMBARKING

Put your bags outside the cabin door the evening before disembarking.

Once again: keep anything you will need the next morning with your hand luggage.

EMERGENCY DRILL

All passengers must take part in the emergency drill, which usually takes place on the day of embarkation. You will find a life jacket in your cabin which you must put on for the drill. You will be informed of the drill on the PA system; proceed to your allocated master station, which is a place near the lifeboats. This is where the actual practice is done.

LIFEBOATS

The number of lifeboats is prescribed by

Heading the dream destination

Tips & tricks for your cruise

Is this your first big cruise? We have collected some info and concepts for you about life on the high seas.

international law and exceeds the maximum passenger capacity by 125 per cent. "Women and children first" does not apply to emergencies; for handicapped persons there are boats adapted to their special needs.

MEDICAL CARE

Cruise ships have medical personnel on board; on the larger ships, there is even a hospital. Any serious case of sickness is transferred to a hospital on land. Find out to what extent your medical insurance covers any medical treatment for which you initially have to pay yourself. In case of doubt, take out appropriate international health insurance.

The gangway leads into the ship

line. Once it has left, you've got a problem.

SEASICKNESS

On the Atlantic, the weather can sometimes change and turn stormy, which will make the going a bit rougher. The stabilisers of modern ships suppress most of the rolling, but in severe cases they cannot completely eliminate it. To be on the safe side, you can buy medication against seasickness at a pharmacy.

SHORE EXCURSIONS

You can book shore excursions, including shuttle buses, on board and join sightseeing trips, for example. But you can also organise your on-shore activities yourself. If you want to go off on our own, you will find taxis in most ports; sometimes you're lucky and can reach the city centre on foot.

BERTHING TIMES

Before going ashore, you will be informed how much time you have available. You must show your boarding pass when leaving and returning to the ship. Note: Allow enough time for your return to the ship. Even though ships wait a while for delayed passengers, sooner or later they have to leave, as extended stays in port incur costs for the shipping

ROADSTEAD

Many ports are too small for large cruise ships to enter. In such cases the ships anchor outside; they ride at anchor "in the roadstead".

TENDER BOAT

Passengers are carried ashore from ships lying in a roadstead by smaller boats, called tenders or tender boats, for their excursions.

DRESS

Although dress rules have become less strict nowadays because of the greater variety of cruise ships, you should enquire what dress code is required on board your ship. As a general rule: the more stars a ship has, the more formal the dress. The dress code for dinner is usually indicated on the board programme for the day. Many shipping lines also publish information on the proper dress style on their website.

CABIN INFORMATION

On cruise ships, there are normally four classes of cabins that differ quite a bit as regards furnishings and price.
▶ **Inside cabins:** These are the cheapest type, without a view of the sea and with rather limited space.
▶ **Outside cabins:** Here the porthole allows you to see the sea, but the cabins are usually not noticeably larger than inside cabins.
▶ **Balcony cabins:** These have their own balcony, which can be an advantage if the weather is fine.
▶ **Suites:** the most expensive category, with better furnishings, more space and additional service.

TIPPING

Many cruise lines charge a flat rate at the end of the trip that is allocated to the crew. Other lines leave it up to you how much you want to tip whom. If uncertain, enquire at your line what their customs are.

ICEBREAKERS

Cruises are also very popular with people travelling alone. For these passengers the lines arrange appropriate evenings where one can get to know other passengers travelling alone. Don't worry, these evenings are not dating occasions!

ON-BOARD ACCOUNT

All purchases made on board are cashless transactions. When you embark, you Index your credit card or pay a deposit. Dollars and euros are the most common cruise currencies. Note that in the case of dollars, conversion fees are charged to the credit card account. You receive your cruise account before you disembark. What you pay afterwards is charged separately.

ON-BOARD PROGRAM AND BUSINESS

On cruise ships, entertainment is provided at appropriate (evening) events. Shops and boutiques are provided for shopping.

ABC OF SHIPPING

Aft – rear part of the ship (stern, poop)

Anchor – keeps the ship in place; cruise ships have several

Bearing – direction of travel of a ship, course

Bell(s) – nautical indication of time in half hours

Bow – front part of a ship

Bridge – place from where the captain steers the ship

Bunker – fuel store (tanks) on a ship

Captain – person in command of a ship

Companionway – narrow stairway inside a ship

Dock – part of a port where a ship moors

Fathom – nautical measure of length; a fathom equals six feet

Flagship – best ship of a shipping line, often also the largest and newest

Galley – ship's kitchen

Gangway – stair or bridge whereby the passengers embark

Heave to – slowing down and changing direction of a ship

Hull – body of a ship, without superstructure

Keel – part of a ship running continuously from stem to stern of a ship and mostly submerged

Knot – nautical unit of speed; 1 knot = 1 nautical mile per hour

Lee – the downwind side of a ship

Luff – the upwind (windward) side of a ship

Maiden voyage – first voyage of a ship with passengers

Master stations – waiting areas at the lifeboats in emergencies

Mayday – international call for help on sea

Nautical mile – nautical unit of measurement, equal to 1852 m / 1.1508 mi

Pier – mooring place for ships (also called a quay)

Pilot – steers the ship through tricky waters

Pitching – Lengthwise up-and-down movement of a ship

Port fee – is calculated in each port on the basis of a ship's size

Porthole – round window

Port side – left side of a ship (looking forward)

Purser – ship's officer who keeps the accounts

Rolling – lateral swinging of a ship

Set sail – to depart from a port on a course

Sextant – nautical measuring instrument for determining position

Sister ships – ships with the same construction and belonging to the same line

SOS – international distress code

Starboard side – right-hand side of a ship (looking forward)

Stern – rear part of the ship (see Aft)

Swell – movement of water caused by wind

Tide – daily rise and fall of the sea level (ebb and flow)

Wake – water trail dragged along by a ship while sailing

Watch – on-duty time of the crew

Waterline – height of the water level measured on the ship's hull

Weighing anchor – raising the anchor before the ship sails

Yawing – not steering a straight course

INDEX

This index lists selected places of interest and worth seeing that are mentioned in this tour guide.

INDEX

CREDITS

WRITE TO US

e-mail: info@marcopologuides.co.uk
Did you have a great holiday? Is there something on your mind? Whatever it is, let us know! Whether you want to praise, alert us to errors or give us a personal tip – MARCO POLO would be pleased to hear from you.
We do everything we can to provide the very latest information for your trip. Nevertheless, despite all of our authors'

thorough research, errors can creep in. MARCO POLO does not accept any liability for this. Please contact us by e-mail or post.

MARCO POLO Travel Publishing Ltd
Pinewood, Chineham Business Park
Crockford Lane, Chineham
Basingstoke, Hampshire RG24 8AL
United Kingdom

1st edition 2020
Worldwide Distribution: Marco Polo Travel Publishing ltd, Pinewood, Chineham Business Park, Crockford Lane, Basingstoke, Hampshire RG24 8AL, United Kingdom. Email: sales@marcopolouk.com
© MAIRDUMONT GmbH & Co. KG , Ostfildern
Chief editor: Stefanie Penck
Authors: Bert Sanders, Karl Teuschl, Gesine Froese, Irmeli Tonollo, Manfred Wöbcke, Birgit Müller-Wöbcke, Michael Auwers
Cartography and pull-out maps: © MAIRDUMONT, Ostfildern
Translated from German by Tony Moen, Mo Croasdale, Susan Jones, Kathleen Becker, John Sykes
Pre-press: trans texas publishing services, Cologne

DOS AND DON'TS 👆

STAKING PHOTOGRAPHS

Take special care when photographing locals!

On many islands the people are quite aggressive even when they just think they're in the picture.

Especially on Jamaica's northern coast, there have been unpleasant incidents in this regard.

CHANGING MONEY ON THE BLACK MARKET

On Cuba, in the Dominican Republic and on Jamaica, changing the respective national currency is expressly allowed only in banks and exchange bureaus licensed by the state.

If you change your dollars nevertheless, your holiday could in the worst case end very suddenly.

UNDERESTIMATING THE SUN

Even if you have lightly pre-tanned or if you never had any problems with the sun on the Mediterranean coast, here the effect of the sun is so strong that you could easily end up looking like a lobster.

SITTING UNDER A COCONUT PALM

No, seriously: Every year ten times more people die from falling coconuts than from shark attacks! If such a nut drops from, say, a height of 30 m/100 ft, it can reach a speed of 80 km/h (50 mi/h) and crack a human skull. To put it bluntly, the nut of a coconut palm is harder than yours.

BUYING EVERY SOUVENIR

Among the many souvenirs there are also some that give animal rights protagonists cause for concern: handbags made from crocodile and snake skins, hides, tortoiseshell products, tortoise shells, rare shells and corals and ornaments made from them.

In any case, importing them into the home country may be strictly regulated.

BEING IN A HURRY

Where you are going, people take things easy.

Don't expect European punctuality and dependability from the locals – they are not accustomed to it, they march to a different beat.

Protesting angrily or impolitely gets you nowhere; instead the locals will be nonplussed or get angry too.

COMING OUT

Homosexual organisations and many websites strongly warn against public displays of homosexual behaviour on Jamaica.

Even same-sex couples holding hands can elicit aggressive reactions.

Be particularly careful at dance hall concerts, as the performers like to incite violence against LGBT in their texts.